	DATE DUE		

BALANCHINE'S
MOZARTIANA
The Making of a Masterpiece

BALANCHINE'S
MOZARTIANA
The Making of a Masterpiece

by
Robert Maiorano
and
Valerie Brooks

FREUNDLICH BOOKS
NEW YORK

Copyright © 1985 Robert Maiorano and Valerie Brooks

Library of Congress Cataloging in Publication Data

Maiorano, Robert.
  Balanchine's Mozartiana: the making of a masterpiece.

  1. Mozartiana (Ballet)   2. Choreography.
3. Balanchine, George.   4. Choreographers—United States
—Biography.   I. Brooks, Valerie, 1939–
II. Title.
GV1790.M69M35 1985   792.8′42   84–13726
ISBN 0–88191–013–9

Published by Freundlich Books
80 Madison Avenue
New York, New York   10016

Distributed to the trade by
The Scribner Book Companies, Inc.

Manufactured in the United States of America

10 9 8 7 6 5 4 3 2 1

6–19–86 — MW — 36129

To the memory of George Balanchine and his work.
ROBERT MAIORANO

*In memory of my mother and for my father and Todd
and my children, Nicholas and Sara,
with love and thanks,*
VALERIE

Acknowledgments

—————————— ⸙ ——————————

I acknowledge all my colleagues, teachers, and friends throughout my career in the New York City Ballet, without whom I could not have found the insight to make this book possible. Many thanks, of course, are for the original cast of *Mozartiana*, who lent me their trust during the initial choreographic period. I also thank my friend and agent Richard Boehm, for his suggestion that I do a book about Balanchine in the first place; Edward Bigelow, for his rare knowledge of "things;" Ronald Bates and his staff and crew, for their cooperation; Maitland McDonagh and Deni Lamont for their unsparing information; photographers, Steven Caras, Costas, Carolyn George, Reed Jenkins, Dominique Nabokov, Robert Sandoval and Martha Swope, for their sensitivity; Laura Fortenbaugh for her brave work with my original manuscript; Valerie Brooks, of course, and Larry Freundlich, Sheila Nealon, and Kathy Bozzuti for their excellent work in making this book. Finally and unfailingly, I thank Susan "Suma" Brown for her love.

A special thank you has always gone to George Balanchine.

Robert Maiorano

Acknowledgment

I want to acknowledge the inspiration of George Balanchine, the help of all the dancers and musicians who took part in *Mozartiana* and those in the administration of the New York City Ballet who gave me their time. For their encouragement, I want to thank my friend and editor, Larry Freundlich, his associates Sheila Nealon and Kathy Bozzuti, and my steadfast agent, Deborah Geltman.

Valerie Brooks

Preface

—————————— ༄ ——————————

    This book illuminates only five weeks in the life of George Balanchine. For the artwork of an artist is what is most essential and interesting about the artist, not the biography of the man. The truest representation is to show George Balanchine assembling a new ballet. I experienced and witnessed this phenomenon quite often. His methods of work were most special. They held a poignancy that led towards an understanding of his art. In the summer before the Tchaikovsky Festival of 1981, after having been a member of his New York City Ballet since 1962, I asked Mr. B. if I could write a book about his next ballet. He granted me the privilege, but told me to be careful: "For dancing is only like dancing and roses are only like roses; one is not like the other." I took heed and wrote simply of what I saw and sensed after leaving each rehearsal. Here is the story of how he made what came to be his last masterpiece, *Mozartiana.*

Robert Maiorano
June, 1984

Introduction

———————————— ৡ ————————————

Balanchine was a genius, one of the most creative spirits of the twentieth century. His brilliance lay in his eye, ear and imagination. Although he spoke simply and eloquently about dance, he seemed to be embarrassed when he did. Look, he would say, my ballets speak for themselves. So if there is any way to understand his accomplishment, it is by looking, by watching him put together a ballet, move dancers around, show, tell a story that illuminates a movement or that relaxes the tension. Here is Balanchine at work, making what was his last masterpiece, *Mozartiana*, in the spring of 1981.

He was the last of a special breed—a man who had lived in three worlds and whose life almost spanned a century. A Georgian, half Orthodox, half Moslem, essentially Oriental, he combined in his experience an aristocratic and artistic childhood in Russia just as it erupted in revolution with a European education in the vibrant and daring twenties of Diaghilev, Picasso, Utrillo, Rouault, Derain and Stravinsky. To this he added America—skyscrapers, and energy, long-limbed girls and wide open spaces. He said New York looked like a cylinder and stars. Having trained as a musician and dancer in St. Petersburg, and as a choreographer in Paris, Balanchine was by the age of 25 an amazingly confident and accomplished artist with a vision that would revolutionize an elitist art form in a country that he had never seen. At the time, Balanchine was sick with tuberculosis in one lung and had been given three years to live. Although it took several years for the New York City Ballet and its breeding ground, the School of American Ballet, to be established, Balanchine always made dances—all kinds; for British revues, operas, Broadway shows and Hollywood musicals—that added further to his breadth and depth. His idols grew to include George Gershwin, Fred and Adele Astaire, Jimmy Cagney and Ginger Rogers.

Balanchine married four times—Tamara Geva, Vera Zorina, Maria Tallchief and Tanaquil LeClerq, all ballerinas—and in his first year after leaving Russia, he lived with Alexandra Danilova, who still teaches at the School of American Ballet. Next in his affection, after music, ballet and ballerinas, were the Italian painters Raphael, Mantegna, Caravaggio and Piero della Francesca. And he loved good food. For a while he cultivated roses at a country house he shared with Maria Tallchief. Those close to him knew he loved hot tubs and housework—especially ironing, probably because it straightened things out, just as in his ballets the most complex patterns are finally "straightened out."

Balanchine's first allegiance was to the Russian Orthodox Church. As a child he liked playing at being a priest, inspired perhaps by his uncle who was archbishop of Tiflis, and he went around blessing things. Throughout his life he attended his church. For Easter he would prepare a feast of traditional Russian food. Other times, he made bread, hearty soups—often borscht, kulitch and pasha—and delicate French sauces. Everything contributed to his ballets being so full of excitement, beauty, tenderness, anguish, joy and humor. Balanchine knew instinctively that an arm curved a certain way, an entrance timed with an instrument, a particular body next to another, would be effective in combination with the music he chose. He was very simple, very pure. This may be why the wonderful dances poured from him so easily. He never got in the way of his inspiration. He just went to work, insisting there were no shortcuts to beauty.

During his time in New York, he spent his days and nights first at the City Center on West 55th Street and later at the New York State Theater which he and Lincoln Kirstein got for their company. Most of his life he lived right in the neighborhood in spacious old airy apartments with big kitchens and simple furnishings. For several years he had a cat, Mourka, bright ginger and white, whom he thought of as the ideal dancer. He relaxed after one a.m. at restaurants with close friends. Most recently they were Dr. William Hamilton, the company's doctor, dancer Karin von Aroldingen and her husband, and Barbara Horgan, manager of special projects. He liked wine and vodka with a warm beer chaser, and if bad Mexican food was all that was available—as when he was filming a ballet for television in Nashville—he'd rave about that. Balanchine wasn't very comfortable with people outside his own world, except Russian friends kept from his first days in New York. There wasn't much time for books, theater and travel, though every day he played the piano.

So, not surprisingly, his life did not explain the work. He had a profound sensitivity to human emotions for every one of them is represented and crystallized in his ballets. Balanchine didn't tell stories; he made poems, parables about love—physical poems. The way, then, to get closer to them is to see him physically at work.

Valerie Brooks
May, 1984

The most a man can achieve is to be able to do.
Georgi Ivanovitch Gurjieff

God creates. I only assemble.
George Balanchine

Prologue

In the spring of 1981 the New York City Ballet would hold a festival in honor of Pëtr Ilich Tchaikovsky. For three years it had been talked of. Many preliminary meetings had been needed to decide exactly what would take place. Rumors abounded. Then in February, at the old-fashioned and almost imperial Russian Tea Room, an announcement was made to the press. But not until May did company members hear ballet mistress Rosemary Dunleavy say on the taped telephone message, which gave them their schedule for the next day: "Mozartiana—Main, two p.m. and four p.m.; Farrell, Andersen; Boelzner, Balanchine, Dunleavy."

George Balanchine was going to return to the first Tchaikovsky music that he had ever used for a major ballet, the composer's tribute to Mozart, Suite No. 4 opus 61, "Mozartiana." The ballet was first performed in Paris and London in 1933, and a year later under the auspices of Lincoln Kirstein on the Warburg estate in White Plains, New York. A new version was produced in 1935 for their American Ballet, and ten years later for Sergei Denham Ballets Russes.

In the Main Rehearsal Hall tall mirrors stretch fifty feet across the front of the studio. The ceiling extends another twenty feet higher. Ib Andersen, the principal male dancer called to this rehearsal, rested his elbows on the wooden barre that encircled the room. His sweet handsome face and clear green eyes were expectant. At the piano, Robert Irving, the company's musical director and principal conductor, sat beside pianist Gordon Boelzner listening to a passage from "Mozartiana." An odd pair—the tall, portly, balding conductor and the thin, thick-haired pianist, sitting stiff-backed and reading the music. Irving plays just enough of each section for Boelzner to understand the tempo he wanted. They look like two music students preparing for an exam. Every so often Irving explains "nasty spots" in his English accent.

From the far corner, next to the freight elevator, Suzanne Farrell enters the studio. She wears a white camisole over a powder blue leotard and pink tights covered by black parachute nylon sweatpants rolled to mid-thigh. Her light-brown hair is pulled into a ponytail. To limber up she stretches on the floor and brings her knees up, legs together, and rocks her hips from side to side, strengthening her stomach, taking pressure from her feet, and stretching her buttocks and thighs all at once. Today she has not wrapped herself in the beautiful black and pink flowered shawl she bought in the Moscow airport many years ago. Balanchine does not like his dancers to cover themselves in warm-up clothes.

Andersen appears tired. His wirey and well-proportioned body is warm; still shining with sweat from a rehearsal of Balanchine's *Apollo*. His curly hair sticks to the sides of his angular face.

On the hour, George Balanchine arrives by the rear door, wearing a faded denim Western shirt rolled to the elbows and navy blue slacks. The shirt looks like a blue sky filled with white clouds. He holds his head regally but his hazel eyes are gentle.

He smiles down at Farrell as he walks, taking small, sure-footed steps to join Irving and Boelzner at the piano. "We'll start with the theme," he tells Irving. This is the place Tchaikovsky began writing the score. Gently Balanchine conducts Irving. Music fills the room. Andersen and Farrell draw close to the piano. Balanchine already hears the full orchestral sound.

"It is Mozart," Balanchine says, facing the dancers; and continues, "Nobody in Russia knew much of Mozart, so Tchaikovsky, who adored him, wanted his countrymen to hear his music. This suite was like an introduction for them.

"We will have to pause here"—Balanchine points to a stop in the music—"we don't want the music to be drowned out by the applause of Suzanne's fans." She laughs and says, "Ib's too!"

With a trace of sobriety, Balanchine walks to the far corner, and the dancers follow. Irving leaves for other rehearsals and Boelzner centers himself on the piano bench. Silence. Balanchine takes Farrell's hand. A ballet has begun.

THEME
AND VARIATIONS
I AND II

Simply, with great delicacy, Balanchine leads Farrell by the hand. Andersen watches them walk to the center of the studio. They stop and return to him. He takes his partner's hand, and starting on the same foot with the exact number of steps, leads her to the same spot.

"Good," says Balanchine, moving quickly to where they stand, and then leads his ballerina straight forward, down the center of the floor, which is the same size as the theater's stage. He inclines toward her. They return to Andersen, and he repeats the same walking step. Balanchine looks to Boelzner. "*Aaand*," he says quietly in his nasal voice. The first measures of music soften the harsh fluorescent light.

"Ta, ta teee, da dum, dum, ta." Balanchine hums the tune, stressing where the accents should be. The dancers understand and the corresponding music is played. Everything fits. But Balanchine suggests, in this new sequence, that Andersen simply walk, crossing behind Farrell, before she dances the last half of her more complicated combination. After they can accomplish this in both directions, the music is repeated.

Satisfied, Balanchine walks to the dancers and faces the mirror, ready to continue. Andersen watches his feet. Farrell is a little off to the side, studying Balanchine's face for signs of what is to come. In the silent studio Balanchine appears to be hearing the music. He moves a hand, bends a knee then retracts both.

As the choreographer dances, he hums the theme. The dancers hear what is coming and step to every beat, keeping time as Balanchine choreographs elegant arm and hand movements, interchanges and switches, behind backs and over heads. They look like lovers taking turns leading each other through a formal garden. After four new sequences are demonstrated and developed, Boelzner plays. At once the steps begin to flow as the dancers become more sure of the movement.

"Okay, from the beginning—for the brains." Balanchine smiles, his eyes excited, full of light.

Everything goes smoothly as Farrell gives occasional tugs to let Andersen know what is next. Amazingly he did not lose time. The most difficult part of learning a ballet is putting together a new sequence with an earlier one. At one point in the music there is one of these dead spots—all three forget what is next. Andersen chuckles. They stand in a huddle, gesturing. Farrell remembers her arm was behind her, but Andersen was on the other side. Was it the other hand he had hold of? Was he on the wrong side of her? If so, how could he have arrived there from the previous step? That step, every-one was sure, was correct. Was she facing the wrong direc-tion? Was he? Was her hand supposed to be behind her at this point in the first place? Was it the other hand? In five minutes they figure it out. If they lost the sequence, it would not have been a disaster, but a shame. Usually Balanchine's initital responses to music are his best. The little dance is charming.

They move on, with Balanchine calling out corrections of "more *croisé*," or "*effacé*," when those body directions are necessary. During this princely march of music, the dancers are separated. Andersen faces front, matching Farrell. He is ready to dance opposite her, but Balanchine corrects. "Just present her . . . thaaat's right," he says, as Andersen gestures toward Farrell.

"She is going to do . . ." Balanchine, at a loss for words, shimmies his hands.

"Oh, that I can do." The ballerina laughs, shaking her hands in imitation of Balanchine, like a Charleston dancer. He smiles broadly. The theme is over. The dance has turned out to be a presentation of Farrell, just as the theme introduces the music which will follow.

Balanchine is quiet. Thirty minutes have passed. Farrell remains standing where he left her, poised, attentive, and vulnerable. He is about to give her a dance. Andersen slides down to the floor. Balanchine stands near and slightly in front of Farrell. Although they don't touch or speak, they seem to be conversing. Their collaboration, their communion, has been a glory of the New York City Ballet for twenty years. Now she is ready for more.

Balanchine extends his right leg and takes the first step onto the ball of his foot. Farrell follows automatically onto the tip of her toe. Her hard-tipped toe shoe supports her on pointe as she balances and waits, towering over him as he chants the beat softly. He checks her position with his head still bowed in thought. She comes off pointe not taking her eyes from him. He repeats the same movement twice, but with his right arm extending over his head, before repeating it to the left. Farrell dances first without, then with the arm movement. When the heavy metal doors open, only Balanchine's eyes flicker.

Thin, pretty, curly-haired Rosemary Dunleavy, assistant ballet mistress of the company, walks to her usual spot behind and off to the side of the dancers. She too remains fixed on Balanchine. But she also watches Farrell's every move for it is Dunleavy's job to memorize every step of the choreographer, and to make sure the dancer has too. Her ten years as a member of New York City Ballet's corps de ballet was perfect preparation for her current role in retaining all the parts of new Balanchine ballets as well as the majority of the entire repertory. Yet this demanding responsibility is only one of her important jobs in the company.

The variation moves smoothly with Andersen watching the three figures glide, step, tap and turn. Farrell is picking up every nuance of Balanchine's inflections of movement. By adding, developing, syncopating and subtracting, Balanchine innovates within the classical tradition. Though striving for newer movement, his respect for the mathematics and historical essence of the music is the foundation of his choreographic technique.

Balanchine steps forward with his right foot, keeping his left foot slightly off the floor behind him. He bends his right knee as he swings his left leg around in the air, touching his foot to his right ankle in one movement. Farrell follows him exactly, using the classic vocabulary: *piqué arabesque, rond de jambe en l'air* to a *plié*, and *coupé devant*. Stepping on his left foot, he repeats himself. Farrell follows and Dunleavy follows her.

"Maybe backwards first, then forwards," Balanchine suggests. After seeing the results, he asks the ballerina to place the foot back as she moves forward, and forward as she moves back.

"Thaaat's right."

Balanchine signals and Boelzner plays, marking *coupés* on the score as a reference point in Farrell's variation.

Farrell has trouble with this sequence when she repeats all of the variation that has been assembled. To sense the stamina of a dancer and the flow of the design, Balanchine always asks to see the continuity of the combinations. Farrell has to stop again and again. She apologizes: "You must have corrected me a dozen times." Balanchine does not comment, but shows her the direction he wants her to move in once again. Farrell has rarely misconstrued one of his combinations.

Finally the music carries her on until she has no more steps, and she waits frozen in her last pose. By remaining like this, she is giving him all a dancer can at this point. Balanchine studies her, then copies her pose, to sense in his own body which direction the weight will fall, or which way the foot in the air might naturally continue to another position in the air, or where and how to step onto the floor. With his musical guide and visual idea Balanchine slowly steps to the floor and kicks the other leg. He then faces Farrell and watches her extend his movement into its balletic form with a straight knee, pointed foot and sharp *battement* of a classical dancer.

He nods agreeably while fiddling with his back as though he is trying to tuck in his shirt, although it is already tucked in. He steps forward and adds a small combination to the previous movement and checks the mirror to see if Farrell has responded. She shows him that she has understood.

Abruptly, he starts dancing in a circle before swinging into a diagonal. Somehow Farrell and Dunleavy stay right with his fervor. He stops and mops his brow, pushing the sweat through his thin white hair. No matter what he is doing he keeps his aristocratic mien—the great cranium with its arched and noble nose and hollow cheeks. Although his eyes have thousands of expressions, he always holds his thin lips in an attentive pout. It is as though he must taste everything that he sees.

"Going on," Balanchine says, hopping from one foot to the other before adding a turn to the same steps. Farrell waits for him to finish experimenting and presents him with his wish.

Balanchine incorporates a raised arm she used naturally in dancing the last step of her variation. On the final two beats, he adds another. She curls her wrists back and forth before placing them on her hip one at a time, as though giving a quick acknowledgment to the audience. As she repeats this for the last time, Balanchine darts to the side of the studio, loops around, runs to center and counts eight beats out loud to the music.

Andersen stands up.

"You come in as she finishes," Balanchine says, turning to the young man. The dancer is already next to him.

Andersen joined the company in 1979, at the age of 25, and he learned the Balanchine style with as much facility as any foreign dancer ever has. In his native Denmark, he had appeared in only two ballets of Balanchine and Jerome Robbins. However, his Bournonville training in the Royal Danish Ballet Academy and company (with Hans Brenaa and Kirsten Ralov) gave him a quick-footed technique which complemented the Russian influence of Edite Frandsen and Vera Volkova. This combination gave him strength, grandeur, and a fluid bearing in his torso, head and arms. Even though he had early success in Denmark—at 18 he was his company's newest *danseur noble*, dancing outstanding performances in ballets by Rudi Van Dantzig, John Neumeier, Harald Lander, and Glen Tetley, it was with George Balanchine and Jerome Robbins that he always wanted to work.

"Ta ta," Balanchine says, demonstrating a jump by merely stepping forward right, left, and leaving the back toe of the left foot to drag behind him for a fraction of a second, before placing the left foot in front of the right and repeating with the hint of a jump, "ta ta." He lets the right foot linger ever so slightly before crossing in front of the left and repeating two more jumps, "ta ta, ta ta."

Observing Balanchine demonstrate these first two *sissonnes*, Andersen immediately jumps, scissoring his legs front to back and landing in the usual heel to toe and toe to heel fifth position, before switching the back foot front and springing once again.

The eager dancer executes four *sissonnes* perfectly, but the timing is faulty. Though more than fifty years younger than Balanchine, Andersen seems to be moving slower. It becomes markedly evident as Boelzner joins in with music. Balanchine's tappings and Andersen's landings have not been synchronized. Andersen has missed an important nuance in Balanchine's demonstrations.

Dunleavy steps forward and comes to their aid with an objective view. But she, also, is wrong, so Balanchine demonstrates once again, though this time at a slower pace. Andersen bounds forward once again.

"Not so big," Balanchine cries out.

Still, it is wrong. Finally, Dunleavy understands and describes the step verbally to Andersen: "It is faster. Don't cross your back foot to fifth position. He wants the foot to *coupé* behind before bringing it forward." She jumps and makes an obvious landing on one foot with the rear leg finishing with the toe touching the floor. Andersen tries and tries this unfamiliar one-footed landing and timing. Eventually, he achieves what Balanchine has demonstrated. The slight variable had initially gone undetected; for Andersen had transcribed from habit what he had been trained to dance whenever a *sissonne sauté* was called for. But what is usual is usually uninteresting to Balanchine. Slightly altering steps from how they are normally done is one way his dances attain their distinction.

As Balanchine sits down in his chair, he winces in pain. He prepares to watch Andersen dance the phrase but soon he lifts himself up and uneasily proceeds to make a new sequence.

While Andersen works, Farrell receives a foot massage from a fellow dancer and reveals, "When I was a girl in Cincinnati, I sang the Ave Verum section of this suite at church, in Latin. At the time I never dreamed that I could possibly be dancing it to Balanchine's choreography." As a child Farrell danced on top of tables and chairs, held recitals in her backyard, and formed a New York City Ballet Fan Club before coming to New York on the recommendation of ballerina Diana Adams.

She sits quietly watching Balanchine work with Andersen. The variation is piquant and brilliant with abrupt changes of movement and direction demanding all of his nimbleness and sharp technique.

After Andersen has mastered the footwork of each challenging combination of steps, Balanchine adds an array of different arm movements. They change the character and line of the basic steps. Some are surprising but embellish the look as vibrato does a note. Laughter fills the space. The complicated instructions have Andersen hopping about and tapping his head and rubbing his stomach in complete befuddlement. Grinning, Balanchine simplifies the combination.

Wanting to give everything he can, the dancer practically explodes with every step. "Jump less. It is faster," Balanchine keeps having to remind him.

But Balanchine, too, is eager; it's in his eyes. Eyebrows arched, lips moving, he checks the score over Boelzner's shoulder, looking like a child peering into a tray of sweets. Having rechecked the new phrase of music, he scurries over to Andersen and turns his back on the dancer so that he will face the same direction, to facilitate Andersen's understanding of the next step.

Balanchine dances toward the piano. "Ta ta tee tat dum," he says while finishing with a jump, turning the right knee in, then out, before landing. Andersen flies after him, dancing a regular *pas de chat*, with both knees bent and facing out to the side in midair. He has not molded himself yet to Balanchine's inflection. Throughout the dance, Andersen's neatness and classical turnout have been exemplary. But his dancing has not been as sensitive as Farrell's reaction to Balanchine's stretching of the classic forms of particular steps. He is still new to the style. Farrell, having worked so closely with Balanchine for so long, always seems to see the accent and verve which Balanchine wants. It always appeared that Farrell stretched and molded Balanchine's steps to her own body. But it was she who understood and did exactly what he gestured, trusting in him totally.

Toward the end of the variation, Balanchine senses Andersen's need to jump and gives him larger leaps. In the beginning, it seemed Balanchine wanted to have Andersen's first variation as delicate as possible. For it would balance Farrell's first variation and also leave room to build. Andersen darts overhead and finishes with a distinctive flick of his wrist. His arm is curved perfectly over his head.

"That's good."

A girl in the corps enters quietly, a few minutes early for her rehearsal of Balanchine's *Vienna Waltzes*. Balanchine teases her about the sweatband she wears around her head.

"You are like Bjorn Borg," he says, which prompts a shy smile. He pauses briefly, satisfied that the theme and first two variations are complete, then: "Now for the brains." The dancers take their starting positions and Boelzner plays the baroque theme.

Other girls walk into the room along with the pianist who will play for the next rehearsal. Farrell and Andersen parade through the theme and follow with the outlines of the day's complicated work. It goes smoothly. The room is warm with smiles as Balanchine rises from his chair. Dunleavy stops him and asks him what hours he would like to work tomorrow.

"Whenever they are free . . . I just hope I can," he says; then, answering her questioning look, "I hurt my back the other day when I was taking my pants off. You know I don't have good balance," he says, miming slipping off his pants and hopping on one foot. Everyone listens closely to these words from their agile mentor.

"And today," Balanchine exclaims, "I hurt my back again, when I put them on!"

9

VARIATIONS
III AND IV

---⋐---

By ten-thirty the following morning, the Main Rehearsal Hall was jammed with dancers, crowded, shoulder to shoulder, along the barre encircling the studio and surrounding five portable barres, ready for their daily class. They twisted hips and torsos in various positions, and stretched in splits. One girl bent forward and split her legs up against a wall, others split their legs sideways, pulling their bodies along each leg or rolling over onto their stomachs. Some used five-pound weights and swung their legs or arms in large arcs. Others warmed up with classical ballet exercises but at tempos to suit their own inner-body rhythm this particular morning. A few just rested on the floor with their feet on a wall. Last night's performance finished fewer than twelve hours ago.

Helio "Sonny" de Soto enters the studio and slips into a chair at the piano, his lanky body a half-foot longer than the six-four baby grand. While sipping coffee he talks in his rich Georgia drawl to those dancers who were using the piano as a surrogate barre.

Company class is not usually this crowded when John Taras, one of the three ballet masters, teaches. Nor are the

10

technically demanding classes of the ex-Bolshoi dancer Andrei Kramarevsky as well attended. The eight apprentices and the newer girls in the company are posing, presenting themselves as prettily as they can. Some wear flowers in their hair. New leotards hug their trim figures, and almost everyone wears toe shoes, rather than the more pliable and comfortable ballet slippers. With Balanchine, toe shoes were de rigueur; and this morning it is Balanchine who is teaching— or so the telephone tape and schedule had said. But recently there had been a number of times when expectations had been disappointed. Over the last three years, a heart attack, a double bypass operation and, only months ago, cataract operations had slowed him down. For years he used to teach the hour class nearly every day, almost always running over. Now it was only one or two a season. The apprentices and a surprising number of company members have actually never had a Balanchine class. When the rear door opens conversation stops and everyone turns.

With one hand holding the other in front of his stomach, he walks toward the front of the room. All one hears is the soft patter of his white Italian moccasins as he makes his way to the piano. He does not banter with the pianist, with Farrell, or with Jacques d'Amboise and Peter Martins, the principal male dancers who usually stand by the piano—just a friendly nod of recognition to leading dancer Helgi Tomasson and de Soto. All have seen whom he has acknowledged. As the music begins, Balanchine's face lights up. It is exhilarating to have him back, choreographing and teaching. He is where he belongs, assuming command to forge his dancers into shape for the Tchaikovsky Festival.

Unlike other teachers, he doesn't specify how many times he wants the first exercise repeated, or if it is to be short *demi-pliés* or full *grand pliés*. Confusion shows on the faces of the apprentices and those new to his classes.

Balanchine can afford this vague start for most of the

dancers know what he wants, and he knows that. The unspoken rule was to do whatever step was requested until he directed otherwise. Of this dedication, he once said to a colleague, "I have to tell them when to stop. Because, if I didn't, they will just keep right on going and never stop."

Holding the barre in their left hands, in first position, the dancers continue to lower themselves, slowly bending their knees until their bottoms almost touch their heels, before rising again at the same tempo. In most classes, these *grand pliés* are done no more than four times in a position. But in his classes there is no routine to exercises or combinations. Experimentation reigns.

After the twelfth *plié*, Balanchine asks the class for second position, making sure the dancers' legs and feet rotate outward from the hip sockets, as is expected in classical ballet. A new girl has the correct "turn out" but holds her legs too far apart and Balanchine stops the class and forces her to place her toe so she would have no body weight upon her heels. This was Balanchine's essential law of dance; weight on the balls of the feet as opposed to the heels, allowed far greater freedom of movement.

All lower themselves a dozen times in *plié* until he asks them to continue in the fifth of the five basic positions. Third was cut since it is merely a less crossed and simpler version of the fifth in which the feet cross one another, touching toe to heel and heel to toe. It is a position that is hardly ever done. But the deletion of the fourth position evolved into a habit of Balanchine's class. He began cutting the fourth position *grand pliés* twelve years ago, when he and Farrell were both having knee problems. Balanchine even used to pray for her knees. With the legs separated, and the feet pointing sideways in opposite directions, an immense strain is placed upon the knees as the body lowers between them. The five basic positions for *pliés* became three. Economy is essential in Balanchine classes. Without any explanation, he asks for a series of exactly placed foot-sliding *tendus* after the *pliés*: "To the side."

De Soto plays a jaunty Noel Coward song, a refreshing departure from Schumann, Schubert, Mozart, and the bits of famous ballet music that all dancers have been weaned on— and which can get on their nerves. The tune is welcomed at the start of the day. Balanchine claps his hands in the tempo he wants. The pianist is playing a little too fast. The slower tempo is relished for many know what is coming. Newcomers had heard tales, and the bodies of the older members had never forgotten. It was the speed of Balanchine; the speed that built this company; the speed that separated a Balanchine dancer from any other in the world. In his classes Balanchine developed that speed slowly.

The *tendus* grow faster with each series of sixty-four, or until he decides to stop or have the dancers switch legs. Usually he stopped and talked, sometimes telling stories so long that the dancers got cold. Today, however, they cannot find their breath. All he wants to do is give them what they need. Each series becomes increasingly faster, preparation for the next. Eight varying speeds with a repetition of at least sixty-four with each leg are barely managed. The most courageous dancers last through a hundred and twenty-eight *tendus* of each leg at the fastest tempo of all. Balanchine believes that relentless repetition is what the body best understands. Only once is there a pause during this escalating drill.

"Did you ever see a mole?" Balanchine asks an apprentice. "No? Well they have no eyes . . . and *still* they know exactly where they go. Your feet have no mind, no eyes, no nothing; but they just know where to go." He makes her correct her *tendus* by having her slide her foot back and forth, making sure the tip of her shoe moves to the precise spots on the floor.

"Feet are like moles!" he announces, before a faster series. The many diversified barre exercises of most ballet classes, such as *pliés*, *tendus*, sharp *jetés*, soft *fondus*, hip-opening *ronds de jambe á terre*, and strengthening *en l'air*, sudden *frappés*, brilliant *battus*, stretching *grand port de bras*, extending *developpés*, controlling *dégagés* and heart-pounding *grand battements* are basic to the beginning of each class, which is in turn preparation for the day ahead. Balanchine's presence in class produces absolute concentration. Today's barre lasts just fifteen minutes. All exercises are deleted except *pliés*, multitudes of *tendus*, and high-kicking *grand battements*. Everything has been done to the side; nothing to the front or back, nothing circular. Finally, when Balanchine says, "Okay, that's enough," the newer dancers wander haltingly from the barre, staring wide-eyed at one another. The short barre is a shock to the body, but it is exactly what is needed—an injection of Balanchine: his spontaneity, his total dismissal of the routine. The classical discipline is all that has remained.

Farrell once said how much she missed his classes when he was sick. She had always given herself additional Balanchine classes during the four years she danced in Maurice Béjart's Ballet of the Twentieth Century in Brussels. "How could one dance a Balanchine ballet correctly without ever having taken a class of his?" she asked.

For Balanchine, classes seemed to be a laboratory for extensive retraining of his already highly trained dancers. With each succeeding class, a dancer attempts to discipline the body to a finer technique, as Balanchine constantly finds new steps, combinations, and ideas to enhance and extend his theories of classical technique. However today, in the center, after the barre, he is content to continue drilling the dancers.

Without a word, Balanchine shows the first step in the center of the studio. He lifts his foot slightly off the floor to his side and pivots slowly around backward on the other foot, then switches legs. "That's all," he murmurs, before asking for two groups of women and one of men.

As the first group of women choose their places across the floor, he leans against the barre along the mirror and signals for music. They unfold their legs to the side with their feet as high if not higher than their ears. Facing Farrell, he tells them to stay eight long counts before they pivot around backward on one foot. It is much slower than what was shown, making the step much more difficult, keeping the even slower pivot in ratio to the eight-count extension. Their legs gradually droop as he unexpectedly makes them repeat it eight times each way. The first group drags themselves to the barre exchanging comments with the second group of women. Seeing what was to come the men begin to stretch themselves.

Balanchine stops the second group of women once. They immediately let their legs fall to the floor. Opening his chest and spreading his long arms wide, he shows the exact position in which he wants the body and arms held.

"People don't see, so you have to show them!" he exclaims.

Then it is time for the group of men. The eight repeats are killing. Even a young dancer, with one of the strongest leg extensions of any of the men, has difficulty. This adagio technique, with its extreme and extended carriage of the leg, has always been more associated with women. Simply, their wider construction of the pelvic bones and different hip sockets make it easier for them to lift their legs higher than their narrower-hipped male counterparts. However, narrow hips give men a straighter alignment from hips to knees to ankles and allow greater ease in jumping.

So much time is spent on adagio work and arms and head positions that there is little time left for the final virtuosic segment of turns and leaps. Wanting to get across his ideas of how the arms should be coordinated with the position of the head, Balanchine tells the new dancers to ask the old dancers to explain his teachings. Time is scarce. A few years ago, he would have expounded for minutes, telling marvelous stories, of stubborn mules, lazy horses, pompous penguins, and old-fashioned dance masters. Today, he does not want to waste any time. There is a sense of urgency in the air, aside from the tension created by his mere presence and power over the dancers' lives.

He orders one quick set of jumps in place before class is over. The initiated dancers are surprised by the unorthodox class; yet it is a great lift to everyone's spirits to have him back. Balanchine waves to a smattering of applause and takes off to his office downstairs.

When he opens the stairwell door, four girls around twelve years old stand before him, white ostrich plumes in their hair, dressed in black, bell-shaped tutus. They are wearing the little Scaramouche costumes from the Balanchine Italian *commedia dell'arte* ballet *Harlequinade*. The costumes look similar to pictures of the corps de ballet in previous versions of *Mozartiana*.

"Here they are, Mr. Balanchine," Mme Sophie Pourmel says sweetly in her Russian accent. Balanchine nods to the energetic woman, who has supervised the women's wardrobe for the last eighteen years. She has spent most of her life in the same role, starting with the Ballet Russe, as preserver, adjuster and taciturn mother of all costumes and those who wear them. Now, still elegant and beautiful, the elderly Mme Pourmel nudges the girls into a straight line so Balanchine can see them all at once. David Richardson, a long-time corps de ballet dancer, in charge of the children who appear in New York City Ballet productions, waits for Balanchine's reaction. The four girls stand rigid under his scrutiny. Balanchine does not like the plumes, and immediately Mme Pourmel plucks all four from the tops of their heads.

"No taller than this one," he states, taking one girl from the line. "Or else I can use my own girls." Richardson takes note.

"But are the costumes all right?" asks Mme Pourmel.

"Yes, of course," replies Balanchine, as he leaves for the sanctuary of his room at the end of the hall.

This kind of brief encounter was usually the best way to approach the elusive Balanchine—placing oneself in the path of his usual route after class or rehearsals. Any company member felt that prearranged appointments brought too much anxiety, making them feel as though they were encroaching on his time. Mme Pourmel had been told about *Mozartiana* only two days ago.

Today's rehearsals have already begun. There are to be twenty-two of them; one is a trio for Andersen and two girls, set to a polka by Tchaikovsky. It is a selection of the many piano pieces that Jerome Robbins is challenging himself with. In Balanchine's estimation, Robbins is the only man in the world other than himself who can see and understand how the scope of the theatrical presentation will require the dance to evolve. Robbins rehearsed his dancers for two hours, while Balanchine, after a half-hour reprieve, took the only rehearsal of *Vienna Waltzes*. This season all one hundred six company members are prepared to perform in the regular repertoire with minimal preparation, due to the enormous amount of time needed to rehearse the new Tchaikovsky works. Incredibly, despite the vast repertoire, dancers rarely forget a ballet they have performed.

Balanchine starts to push the piano away from the wall to give himself space to stand while looking over the pianist's shoulder. Instantly, Boelzner reminds Balanchine of his bad back, and shoves the piano himself, while Balanchine stands aside following the music.

"Maybe you should have some sound," Boelzner suggests, referring to the common company use of ultrasound wave therapy for muscle spasms. Balanchine twists and winces in pain, nodding, his eyes still on the music.

As they read the score, Farrell and Andersen enter from opposite doors at the exact time. Farrell is in a clean set of practice clothes. She knows it is not pleasant for her or her partner to dance in wet leotards. In the past, Balanchine gave different ballerinas individual perfumes—not to disguise their perspiration, but to give each a distinctive aroma. One imagines that in his journeys through the theater, Balanchine came upon a certain fragrance and delighted in pausing and calling to mind the dancer to whom he'd given the perfume.

Boelzner plays yesterday's variation with Balanchine looking over his shoulder. Meanwhile the two dancers take time to review their steps. Balanchine is leading Boelzner to interesting places in the upcoming music.

Spread-eagled on the floor, Andersen and Farrell rest from the run-through and from previous rehearsals, in anticipation of the work ahead. Balanchine mentions going over the score with Robert Irving tomorrow, before scurrying to the center of the room. The two rag dolls come to life and stand tall. Balanchine is eager to play. But as he approaches the ballerina, Boelzner interrupts him.

"Wouldn't you like to see what you did yesterday?" he asks. Only Boelzner, Balanchine's trusted and experienced pianist, would dare make such a suggestion.

"Oh, okay," says Balanchine, drawn out of his thoughts. The pianist plays the allegretto music and Andersen and Farrell repeat what they have just reviewed, with the added buoyancy that music brings. Even yesterday's tricky spots are danced easily under Balanchine's curious eyes.

Sara Leland enters the studio. Her driving, courageous and playful onstage personality is now subdued. In medium-heeled street shoes and her practice clothes, she is not here as a principal dancer but as Dunleavy's assistant. She places a pad and pencil on the floor and watches intently. It is the first time, in recent years, that anyone other than Dunleavy has recorded a new ballet by Balanchine. Leland has usually notated Robbins' work.

The music stops; Balanchine faces Farrell and tells her to

continue on Andersen's last step. Balanchine rises up on the balls of his feet as in the first variation, but brings his right foot in front of his left ankle and kicks it out sideways, before turning around with his white moccasins digging into the floor. Farrell replies. He leads her in a diagonal toward center. She starts to walk high on pointe in a larger circle, expanding from the previous turn around herself. The asymmetrical designs are very characteristic of Balanchine. Andersen recognizes the beginning of a new variation for the ballerina and slides down against a wall to rest.

The ensuing steps are intricate and small, yet contain the same level of energy Balanchine has had ever since class. Balanchine's sensitivity to the new music reflects in Farrell's movements. Although his face rarely reveals that he has discovered remarkable steps, Farrell appears to watch him think. When she studies him closely enough, she can see satisfaction in his eyes, then switch concentration to his feet and body. One can see the pencil of a recently-arrived journalist, John Corry, move briskly across the page and come to rest. He looks on.

The two silent figures begin to demonstrate for each other. Slowly interweaving, the choreographer requests nuances of gesture to the dancer's every movement, and the dancer responds in turn. These may be Balanchine's favorite moments, watching his picture step out of his imagination, adding strokes of new thought.

Moving backward along a diagonal, the figures prescribe a circle. "Count in fives," he says, and signals for the music.

Boelzner plays the *poco meno* variation on the theme. It sounds as if it skips a beat in syncopated time. The odd count of five is theoretically incorrect, for it is actually a common 4/4 time. However, a five seems easier to hear, especially when dancing at full speed. Dancers and musicians usually count the same music differently, with dancers counting to the slower beat of the tempo and musicians to the faster beats within the measure. Quite often dancers count differently from one another, usually corresponding to their own particular movements. These different counts can be very confusing when one dancer overhears another quietly counting during a performance. Sometimes it is done on purpose.

Now, with Balanchine counting the music out loud in fives, Farrell dances with ease what she has tried time and again. Balanchine starts to move forward, quietly dancing in his head. Abruptly he stops and faces Farrell.

"Can you jump?" he asks, pointing to her foot, alluding to yesterday's sore metatarsals.

"Yes."

Knowing a dancer never wants to admit that something can't be done, Balanchine asks, "Are you sure?"

"Yes, if it's on two feet," Farrell says with a beguiling smile.

Looking like a little boy who has just been given permission to play outside, this 77-year-old man hops forward as though on a pogo stick. Farrell follows without any sign of pain, hopping after him gleefully.

Dunleavy enters, covered in her usual layers of practice clothes and tight toe shoes. She has just returned from conducting a rehearsal of Balanchine's two-act version of Mendelssohn's *A Midsummer Night's Dream*. Her shoes squeak as she walks to her place in the back of the room, keeping her eyes on the romp in the middle of the studio. It is surprising that she has never taken the rewarding option of discarding her toe shoes when she finished her dancing career. They may make her feel closer to the dancers.

Soon Farrell breezes through a complicated combination with unflappable demeanor, leaving both Dunleavy and Leland in awe. But in the last combination of this short variation, Farrell cannot absorb what Balanchine has designed. She runs forward switching fifth positions with intermittent reverse crosses. Both Dunleavy and Leland flash ahead while Farrell has her troubles. Balanchine rerolls his cuffs and smiles at her. It is basically a series of little *pas de bourrées* forward, down on the first foot then three quick crossing steps on pointe. But Balanchine has made it more interesting by pausing for the fourth beat, switching the front leg back while the body is propelled forward. Farrell's feet are moving with the habit which years of study have induced. They are performing like perfect "moles."

Balanchine has just done what is most distinctive in his work. With absolute confidence and a desire to extend the classic idiom of ballet, he takes it to what has been commonly called neoclassicism by changing nuance and timing. He has built upon it for sixty years and it is now classic itself. To Farrell the combination is merely a challenge. The pause after the fourth beat is just long enough to break the continuity, requiring her to remember what leg goes where next. To the observer, the extra pause of a beat gives clarity to the speedy movement, yet it is almost impossible to see. She tries unsuccessfully time and again.

"Even Barnes won't be able to figure it out," Balanchine jokes, referring to dance critic Clive Barnes.

Farrell asks to try it once again. Balanchine watches bemused by her struggle.

"Don't worry, dear. We have two computers," he says. Dunleavy and Leland beam.

Dancing a quick jump to finish, Farrell asks if she is to land on the last beat in the variation.

"We have missed the boomps at the end of the variation because to finish on them is obvious—but now everyone will expect. But we will surprise. We will finish on it this time."

Balanchine delights in surprise; it stimulates his sense of humor. It is one way he challenges himself. For there is no one at the New York City Ballet to challenge his work, to say, "That is no good, George. I think you need to work on it more, maybe try this way or that way." So he has to strive for self-improvement, change and growth alone. If he has a good time doing it, so will many others; if they don't, it doesn't matter. By now he has accomplished what he feels is needed: he knows there are always ballets of his that will be enjoyed if others fail.

Farrell runs through her variation for the last time and Balanchine walks to the left side of the room. He stands exactly where he wishes Andersen to begin his second variation, to save the dancers the expense of coming to him. Andersen stands just behind the choreographer. Farrell again finishes her second variation with a mistake, but no one worries; everyone knows it will be danced right by performance time.

Boelzner, sensing Balanchine's eagerness, continues playing, and the ballet master dashes to the center of the floor where Farrell has been and jumps, bending his right knee. Andersen copies his movement, jumping higher. Balanchine stops and watches Andersen once, then taps out the correct accent in the timing of the feet. Andersen understands immediately and executes it well. The choreographer has made, at the start of Andersen's variations, a graduation of one of Farrell's combinations, by extending it to the air.

Andersen repeats with the music and Balanchine continues with two steps in the opposite direction, before hopping onto both feet and quickly churning his right index finger in the air, signifying turns to the right. "Ta ta ta ta ta ta ta ta ta ta ta ta ta ta ta ta ta ta ta tum," he spins out endlessly.

Everyone bursts out laughing at this impossible request that is the kind of superhuman feat every dancer dreams of. Balanchine is waiting. Andersen gets up his courage and performs the jumping step, with Dunleavy and Leland marking the brilliant beating of his legs with their hands. After a short preparation, Andersen spins out eight pirouettes. When he stops, grinning, he says, "Never again."

Still smiling broadly, Balanchine tells a story in his nasal singsong voice. "I remember Églevsky, fantastic turns. But in

the Glazunov *pas de deux*, he couldn't turn. When I choreographed, I was so excited; here, finally, I had a great dancer
who could turn and turn. So, at the end of his variation, when
the music goes ta ta dum, ta ta dum, ta ta dum ta; I made him
start turning on the silence for four counts before the music
catches his turns, tum ta ta tee tum dya dum tum. In rehearsals, fantastic. But in performance, he never once did it
right. He started only on the last four bars and did just four
turns. Not very interesting." Balanchine raises his arms high
and lets them drop, slapping his thighs with an exaggerated
sigh. "Only Jacques understood what I wanted," referring to
Jacques d'Amboise, the successor to many of Eglevsky's roles.
Once again Balanchine hums the ending of the famous *Pas de
Dix* variation, twirling his finger continually during the break
in the melody all the way through to the end.

Everyone present had seen André Églevsky dance, except
for Andersen. This story was like another of Balanchine's, of
his and Églevsky's first meeting, at the original School of
American Ballet on Madison Avenue at 59th Street. Églevsky,
a powerfully built, long-limbed young man who had trained
under the great Alexander Volonine and Nicolas Legat in
Paris, came to Balanchine in need of work. "I hear you can
turn," Balanchine said.

"Yes," replied André.

"Let me see," said Balanchine.

"But I need money. I am hungry."

"Okay. Turn and you get your money."

The great dancer began with a grand sweeping gesture
with his arms, down into *plié* and then whipped around
twenty-five times, finishing on a dime, with his hand held out
before him. Balanchine gave him a quarter, enough for a
hearty meal at that time.

Now taking his variation from the beginning, Andersen,
slightly off balance, hops once during his multiple pirouettes.

This imperfection would have been detected only by a trained eye. His feat creates another stir—even Andersen can't believe it. No one has ever seen him turn so well.

Balanchine leads him to the other side of the studio with another leap that lands in the middle of the repeating music. Andersen is asked to turn on the remaining phrase before starting a new one with a quicksilver leg-beating combination. Balanchine and Andersen work, one before the other. They are conversing much more fluently today than yesterday; perhaps because this variation, though technically more difficult, is less tricky and easier to learn. The steps and their continuity are a little larger and more in accordance with Andersen's training.

Every time Balanchine has Andersen return to the beginning of the variation, to make sure it isn't forgotten and to discover how it gels, the multiple pirouettes fill the designated music. Andersen's ease assures everyone that he will not miss it in performance either; for what usually gives a dancer technical trouble from the first rehearsals will give the dancer difficulty when performing. The reason is that no matter how much one has practiced what takes over in the strain of performance is the knowledge of having failed before, along with the tendency of the body to revert to primitive habits of structure and training.

When Balanchine has finished building Andersen's variation back toward the original left side of the floor and pauses momentarily to think what to do next, Farrell asks his permission to leave. She whispers to him, pointing to yesterday's sore foot. There is only a half-hour left, and it would obviously be devoted to the rest of Andersen's variation. Tonight she is to dance a demanding role, her second performance of *La Source*. Balanchine understands her anxiety and nods. Farrell gracefully gathers her dance bag and asks Boelzner if the tempo of her "*Mozartiana*" tape is all right, before sweeping out the back door. Balanchine looks after her, nodding his head in exaggeration, playing the role of humble servant.

Turning again to Andersen, and his trusted computors Dunleavy and Leland, Balanchine continues to assemble the fourth variation of Tchaikovsky's theme. He starts with fast beating combinations in circles, a series of double-turns-to-*arabesque*, traveling backward in a diagonal, and little turning jumps into larger springs coming forward. Within twenty minutes, Balanchine ends the variation with Andersen spinning in a last set of multiple *pirouettes* to the repeating theme. Only this time, he has the dancer finish on his knee, and before a final "bump" that Tchaikovsky added to Mozart's music.

Andersen dances the variation through. What a find he is for the company. His arms are quite eloquent, especially for a dancer trained in the Bournonville school of rigid and symmetrical upper torso and head movements that rarely allow lyricism. The rest of his body and his well-shaped legs are equally pliable and not so regal or theatrical as to be limiting in any way.

After a second run-through he drips sweat as he stands around the piano after the rehearsal. He waits while Balanchine and Boelzner discuss their plans to go over the whole score with conductor Robert Irving.

"Mr. Balanchine, how many more variations are there?" Andersen asks.

"Two more for each of you," Balanchine replies. Andersen smiles wanly.

"Oh, it's kind of like the conversation dances in *Chaconne*," Dunleavy pops up. Balanchine does not respond. These variations are much longer than those in the Balanchine/Gluck ballet, *Chaconne*, which are also danced in a continuous pattern, though with both principal dancers remaining onstage.

Andersen drags himself out the front door, followed by the silent reporter.

*   *   *

In the evening's performance Suzanne Farrell is fascinating. She is brilliant. She seems so relaxed and in control, with no sign of fatigue or a faulty foot. She played with the audience, toying with the steps. Older than all the girls onstage, she seems the most lighthearted young woman in the world, perfectly matching the sweet melodies of Delibes' *La Source*. Peter Martins, her partner, is also dancing beautifully; yet he seems preoccupied—probably by the ballets he is choreographing.

From the wings one could see a small stack of tall plastic tubes, enclosed in more plastic, standing behind in a corner of backstage left. They awaited the Tchaikovsky Festival.

VARIATIONS
V, VI AND VII

⸎

At the next morning's class, while truces are being made with aching muscles, Balanchine explains that Capezio is going to be much better because, he had been informed, it would have Italian shoemakers once again. After this welcome interlude Balanchine signals the pianist, and the dancers repeat an exercise with their left legs while Balanchine inspects the lines. He singles out the slightest imperfections with the eye of a master machinist, carefully checking the stress points of complicated machines running at high speed. The faster the feet are placed into exact positions the clearer the movement will be seen by an audience.

As the class progresses, the speed intensifies. By repeating the same movement, the body can remember the correct feeling. At one point Balanchine prompts laughter by imitating the current style of teaching elaborate combinations at the barre—which forces the mind to decipher rather than let the body absorb. It is the accent of time that is varied in Balanchine's class, not the steps. The importance lies in dancing against the music as well as with it, or sometimes even ahead or behind it. However, on this morning the challenge is merely keeping up with it. Yesterday everyone had expected it and matched him. Now he is already ahead, forcing each individual to surpass himself. He slyly mentions, "Those who can't, or are old, don't have to do." He always led the dancers beyond themselves one way or another.

The pace seems impossible, but in most cases the dancers keep up. Even with his suspicion that Americans in particular are sleepy, Balanchine loves their vibrancy. Europeans find it in America and Americans find it in New York. Balanchine was born with it in his Georgian blood. And he demands and uses it. His schoolmate Alexandra Danilova says that the first time she saw the 9-year-old Balanchine, he was darting around a studio in the St. Petersburg school. Speed always distinguished him: he could finish complete masterworks in days, famous dances in hours or classic sequences in minutes.

At the end of the hour Balanchine has a chance to rest with a cup of coffee and talk to Barbara Horgan, his long-time personal assistant. Her office, shared with ex-dancer and now manager Edward Bigelow, is like all offices in the theater, accessible to anyone connected with the company. Glistening with sweat, the dancers have their coffee in rare, undisturbed peace as they traipse by to the next office, to receive their paychecks from company manager Patricia Avedon Turk.

Fueled and primed, Balanchine is ready to begin. It has been a short day as far as rehearsing goes. But since he has supervised almost everything planned or executed in the theater, his day has been full. And the previous evening he watched the performance from his usual spot in the wings, downstage right. In preparation for tonight, Balanchine has coached Andersen in Stravinsky's *Apollo* before the Tchaikovsky rehearsal.

In the Main Hall the only sound is the piano as Richard Moredock skims through the piano score for *Mozartiana*. Farrell enters and takes a few steps high on pointe, testing a new pair of toe shoes, then asks Moredock to play her variation. Obediently, he finds Boelzner's penciled cues and begins as

Farrell marks her first sequence. She moves on time, covering the approximate amount of space, only alluding to the actual steps, as she focuses on the sequence of combinations, not the execution. Andersen arrives near the end of her first dance and continues with his variation, suggesting the steps and spacing, but exacting the definitive timing of the music.

They finish, pleased they do not have any difficulty remembering. Their dances have been intricate, especially Andersen's first and Farrell's second. She mentions she has been twitching in her sleep at night. As a fellow sufferer, Andersen laughs knowingly. Each twitch belongs to a different step.

Almost as if he has known that the dancers need to clear their heads before filling them again, Balanchine arrives ten minutes late. He nods and walks over to his pianist.

"I heard 'Mozartiana' this morning on the radio," he announces, and everyone draws close. He scrunches his shoulders and squints his eyes, pauses and says, "AWFUL. . . . It was some Swiss orchestra, something. I don't remember who, but AWFUL. The minuet was so slow." He closes his eyes and leans his head to the side. "The variations—bad. And the finale, so fast!" he says, crazily blowing an imaginary horn and staggering around on one foot. "Nobody could play it. I don't know how they did it. For that, they were fantastic. But awful, awful. Something Swiss."

As he calms down, he joins Moredock on the piano bench. "Doesn't matter now." The score before him is pacifying; it is marked with the composer's tempi.

Quiet reigns as Balanchine mutters to Moredock, pointing to a place in the music that was destroyed by the Swiss.

Rising, he takes hold of Farrell's hand and walks to the opposite side of the studio. Facing diagonally toward the center, he steps up to fifth position *relevé*, moves forward, then suddenly stops. He stays motionless, thinking. Eventually he steps down on his right foot and brings his other to his knee, before looking back to Farrell and twirling a finger in the air.

"Turn," he says, and turns once himself. After showing the preparation step with the correct timing, Farrell presents him with a double turn. It seemed he wanted only a slow single, but he does not appear to mind, or he would have mentioned it. She repeats the combination along the diagonal, then once again as he scoots after her, suggesting one arm, the other, until deciding both should go over her head and finish on her hip.

Balanchine asks for the music, and Farrell goes around twice slowly, effortlessly. The next to the last time, she skids around in fifth position, unintentionally having come off pointe.

Placing his foot down from the knee into fifth position, and twisting around once in place, Balanchine asks for a *soutenu* after only one turn from Farrell. The new step allows a continual twist from one turn to the next. She pirouettes on pointe and he asks her to twist once off pointe, an odd variation to this otherwise conventional combination.

"Good," exclaims the ballet master, before drawing into himself for more. He blocks out the next step, whistling to himself ever so faintly. He always made this melodic buzz. It was his private music and if a dancer listened closely, he could more fully realize a given step or anticipate what might come next.

Farrell appears self-contained, yet follows intently when walking in a circle with cranelike elegance. Balanchine suggests two *piqué arabesques*, and she follows the direction he was facing. He asks her to lower her back leg—as he had told Andersen not to jump so high. The step immediately takes on a different look from her usual languor. It is concise. Like the classical Mozart contained within the voluptuous orchestration of Tchaikovsky.

A special harmony had grown by this third day of rehearsal

—security in understanding and a shared spirit. Everyone
here was connected by the music and their dedication to
wonderful dances. Richard Moredock, winner of numerous
music competitions, would figure out the tone and timing. He
is a young teacher and coach, greatly appreciated for his abil-
ity to make piano transcriptions of orchestral scores. All
through the years Balanchine too had made piano reductions
of orchestra pieces. For the rehearsals it had been decided to
use the Mozart pieces on which Tchaikovsky based his suite.
Balanchine was weaned on Tchaikovsky when he first studied
the piano as a child, and he used his music extensively in his
choreography. Mozart he used far less: he thought dances to
most of his music would be extraneous because it would be
impossible to ornament his divine perfection. Farrell, who
had danced almost thirty years and spent her first seven
dreaming about the New York City Ballet, was one of the few
ballerinas to have received such devoted attention from Balanchine. For ten years Dunleavy danced every Tchaikovsky
ballet in the repertoire and preserved every one of Balanchine's in her head and body since then. Leland, shadowing
behind, studied ballet from the age of 5 in Boston and danced
with the Boston Ballet and the newly organized Joffrey
Ballet, before joining the New York City Ballet the same year
as Dunleavy, in 1960. Andersen had a strong bond, too, although he had been with the company only one year. The
Bournonville training he had had in Copenhagen was an out-
growth of the same Maryinsky school in St. Petersburg that
produced Georgi Balanchivadze. Years of dance and its history were present in this studio.

As he moves backward, Balanchine takes large steps on an
off-balance angle, kicking his legs behind him. Farrell tries to
follow but has a great deal of difficulty. He doesn't give in,
and adds a few arm movements and a full turn. Eventually
the sequence takes shape with a surprising suspension of
balance.

31

Balanchine is working slower, taking infinite care with this fifth variation. Pausing often, he hunches his shoulders and stares at the floor as though it held the answer. The only sound is the buzz of the fluorescent lights. Farrell poses like a painter's model, in the same line he has last drawn, making it easier for him to extend the form or embellish it. Dunleavy and Leland begin to waver from waiting. The lull passes and Balanchine shoots both feet forward and hops again. Stopping, he faces Farrell and steps forward, crossing his hands, elbows straight and says, "*Brisé.*"

Farrell immediately jumps, "reaching" her legs with straight knees ahead of her before landing and jumping into another leap holding a second with both legs curved behind her in the quintessential flight of *La Sylphide*. The choreographer points to widely spaced spots on the floor where he wishes her to land from each consecutive jump, before stepping back to see an improved version. Farrell has changed to a girl playing hopscotch.

Moredock plays. The step does not look quite the same.

"No," interrupts Balanchine, turning to the pianist, "you must play like a violin." The pianist stares blankly. "She has the wrong accent. It should *not* be even. It is like du ya de ya da yi dee ta ta da dee la yup," Balanchine says, waving his arms around in the air before winding down to wringing his hands. "With accent not even," he stresses, repeating the same phrase again but stepping with lumbering steps to each beat in imitation of the lugubrious sound just heard. Moredock responds with a strong accent in the beginning and then runs the phrase with dexterity. The new combination gains the verve Balanchine wanted.

He steps out twice into a *piqué pirouette* and wavers as he faces Farrell. "Don't turn like me," he says, staggering around with his arms flailing and his eyes rolling. Everyone laughs, and he returns to his chair.

"I can't see," he says in a quieter voice. "This side," he says, pointing to his left eye, "can't see sideways, and forward, and very little . . . like tunnel. The other eye is like regular eye for old man."

The group smiles weakly. No one knows how good or bad his eyes really are, or were. When he returned after his cataract operations last season, the stage lights were darker than anyone remembered them. The ballets with the bright white light and the blue sky backdrop—trademarks of the company—seem much dimmer now. Either Balanchine is able to see better, or his eyes are extra sensitive to light. How much has he missed before? It has always seemed he never misses a thing. The choreographer has begun also to show a greater interest in details. This kind of interest first became apparent after his heart bypass operation last year. It seems as though he wants to fix everything before he dies. Now, as Balanchine watches Farrell twirl into a more surprising version of the *pirouettes*, his love of newness and invention in life is evident.

After a large *arabesque*, more developed than the earlier concise ones, Balanchine finishes her variation with a minute foot-crossing and small jumping combination. It produces an effect similar to the finish to her first variation, except Balanchine has added *pas de chat*. Farrell performs this delicate hop with a grand smile. She then repeats her variation with much concentration, after Leland's memory saved one combination from oblivion.

Boelzner enters. He walks with the palms of his hands habitually facing behind him; it gives away his life spent at the piano—it is the look of an overworked hired helper. The rehearsal is only half over but it is time for Moredock to play for another rehearsal.

"Well, we'll finally have the music played right for a change," quips Farrell out of the side of her mouth so Moredock can hear. For a moment, the joke breaks the pressure of the work.

Balanchine has remained serene. Noticing his concentration, Andersen rises from the floor and limbers quickly. Farrell sits down with her pale blue eyes staring at nothing. "Are we on six?" Boelzner asks. The ballet master nods and glances at the music, checking the sixth variation before walking to the opposite side of the room. Andersen, Dunleavy and Leland gather near the quiet man, giving him space.

Turning to Dunleavy, Balanchine indicates the first series of steps and moves toward the center. In the next combination, Balanchine turns slowly while keeping the alternating accent in the *poco meno* rhythm of the music. It is similar to a simple czardas step with the weight of the body on one foot as the other pushes around. Andersen accomplishes it in time, turns about at the correct speed, but does not have the accent. He is too light. He is not using the floor. Dunleavy shows the step to Andersen after he has tried and failed a number of times.

"Just paddle around, like this," she explains, turning in place, while watching Andersen copy her at the same time.

"Thaat's right," Balanchine exclaims. While Balanchine decides what will be next, Andersen joins the two combinations. The folk dance step of the second combination, danced in ballet shoes instead of boots, automatically gives the step refinement, classicism. Farrell remains immobile, though in a split. She looks withdrawn and unapproachable, her eyes vacant, yet seeing something. Only the faintest movement of her lips reveals that she is merely rehearsing her steps in her mind.

Balanchine continues working, explaining the following combinations to Dunleavy. Andersen still appears an outsider in his variation. It is surprising, since the turns he did yesterday made the choreographer feel that Andersen could do anything he asked. Yet today Balanchine barely notices him. Andersen shows no annoyance. It is possible Balanchine wants to get everything out as quickly as he can, and feels more secure with Dunleavy's experience in translating what he wants to the relatively new dancer.

However, Andersen does move at Balanchine's pace in the following combinations of four *entrechat quatre* and two *entrechat six* turning in place before hopping in circles from one leg to another. Only the dancer's neat positions make the beating legs and crossing feet a pleasure to watch. For when he turns, as he has been asked, all the bad angles might be seen by the audience. But then Balanchine knows Andersen's brilliant beats would look good at any angle; and in a sense, he is showing him off by presenting the steps in a more interesting way than the usual front view.

After learning the next combination from Dunleavy, Andersen shows it to Balanchine. His face is impassive. The characteristic lack of response prompts the dancer to repeat it. Each time he goes through it, Balanchine taps out the time, or suggests a gesture with an arm. Andersen works with thoroughness and speed until Balanchine exclaims triumphantly or smiles wide as a clown.

Balanchine is pleased with the movements he has enmeshed within the music. To get this look of pleasure, most dancers would give their blood. And, it seems that is exactly what Andersen is doing. His green polo shirt is shades darker. Yet with his natural lightness of technique, he still looks buoyant. When the dancer doesn't immediately understand an inflection of movement that Balanchine has just motioned, the choreographer looks surprised. It is so natural to him. It is as though he never violates a dancer's natural way of moving. When he picks a dancer for a new ballet, it is not for his technical abilities, for he assumes those. He looks for particular personal characteristics that will best present his ideas. When Balanchine decided to do *Mozartiana*, he felt that the young Dane was Mozart.

Andersen is now challenged with consecutive *cabrioles*

front and back that move along a diagonal in alternating directions. Balanchine explained on the first day of rehearsals that the jumps would get bigger as the variations progressed. Well here they are, one after the other, and without the aid of any preparatory step.

The dancer remains as he landed, with his right leg behind him, standing on his bent left leg. Balanchine, assuming the approximate position, thinks for a moment then bends his left leg deeper while reaching back with his right foot before stepping and twisting around to the right and landing on his right foot, facing front again.

"*Coupé jeté*," he explains, and Andersen throws his right leg high into the air as he hits the desired line. With the impetus of that twisting jump, Balanchine moves to his right and beats out a complicated rhythm. This quick-stepped combination takes the longest to assemble, decipher and execute properly. Ten minutes later, the variation is complete, with Andersen neatly polishing off a consecutive single, double *tour en l'air*, finishing splendidly on his knee.

As usual in Balanchine ballets, the steps by themselves are not the most difficult part. It's the pace, precision, brief preparation and wide use of space that are unusual; consequently, the dancer must learn constantly and dance automatically as never before. Balanchine often slightly distorts the dancers' line to give a more exaggerated illusion; sometimes a simple thrust of the pelvis displays the body as classically sexy.

Unceremoniously, Balanchine smiles, then turns away from his panting dancer and walks to the piano. A half-hour remains of the two-hour rehearsal. Farrell has kept herself warm with intermittent exercises at the barre so she will still be pliable for Balanchine's choreography. She also has to be ready for her evening performance. Sidling up to Andersen, she remarks on his "killer" variation. He smiles modestly.

Balanchine repeats his story of the abominable Swiss orchestra to Boelzner before he asks that the seventh variation be played in order to set his tempo. It maintains the same 4/4 time and recent air of excitement. The dancers sense it. Farrell, Leland and Dunleavy enjoy themselves by marking steps and variations with their hands. Hundreds of imaginary turns and multitudes of consecutive *tours* and beats flicker between their hands as they join in Balanchine's virtuoso mood.

Dancers love fantasizing impossible feats that require no gravity or other natural restrictions. All have dreams of dancing on the moon and leaping a hundred feet in a single bound, or turning nonstop for hours, or flying off bridges and over buildings, setting records like *entrechat million*. However, when listening to music, dancers stand idly by, knowing that their next steps will obviously be limited by their mere physical capabilities and not described by the wonderful pictures in their imaginations.

Balanchine rises from the piano bench. Farrell stands alone where she finished. The choreographer walks past her a few feet. It is understood this is where she will begin her next dance. Balanchine remains still. He looks mellow. He has stopped sweating. The glint in his eye from challenging Andersen is gone, yet he still has a sense of urgency to give Farrell whatever he can. She has not taken her eyes off him.

With small running steps, Balanchine quietly moves to the center of the rehearsal studio. He once again *bourrées*. Farrell follows. From high on the balls of his feet he lunges forward, leaning and reaching low for the floor. She imitates his movement.

"*Penché*," he corrects. Immediately her back leg swings up as though caught in an updraft; hers is one of the smoothest movements in ballet. Balanchine has her keep her leg fully extended to the ceiling, as she leans over her bending supporting leg. "People shouldn't miss it," he remarks.

Holding his stomach like a Chinese peasant, he leans forward indicating the *penché* and shuffles his feet around. As he stands up, he indicates a position by jutting his left foot forward. Everyone watches Farrell's lithe body slowly rotate on one leg into the new position with her backbend as deep as her *penché*. Balanchine has her continue to the left, before dancing the sequence with the music.

"That's right!" he exclaims as she responds perfectly to the music, automatically phrasing as he desired, using twice the time another might dance the step.

Together Farrell and Balanchine weave the next combinations into patterns. Their harmony is closer than in the first variation when she seemed to be having more trouble picking up and demonstrating the steps. "For some reason, Tchaikovsky gets very loud here," Boelzner booms in imitation, before playing the next musical phrase.

"I know," says Balanchine, stopping his work and walking to the piano. Boelzner pounds out the double fortissimo with Balanchine standing over his shoulder. The choreographer's eyes sparkle. As Balanchine hurries to Farrell, Boelzner concedes, "I suppose it is a good contrast." Boelzner had questioned the fortissimo and suggested the phrase might be softened to blend with the rest of the variation.

But Balanchine, delighted with the upcoming fortissimo, makes a great whirling motion, whistles and swoops his arms down and around and up. The momentum sends him partway around on one leg with both knees touching. Farrell responds by turning once *en attitude* with a boldness that extends what Balanchine has indicated. He corrects her direction, before going on in the same vein, asking for difficult inside *fouettés*. The ballerina easily spins out these turns with her free leg whipping into a sideways position.

The music soon grows powerful again, and Balanchine faces it by asking for a large jump with legs splitting in the air. With these last few combinations, Balanchine has not lost sight of the underlying qualities of the musical variation and keeps within its original baroque style. Tchaikovsky has made a variation on a variation of the theme, with these outbreaks of power.

In the final combination Balanchine is a little more obvious about what he has done by having his ballerina dance a series of soft-kicking *fondus* in a circle. When she dances them with regal aplomb she is like a can-can dancer in Louis XVI's court. Balanchine was never afraid of the incongruous and ironic.

There are only two more bars of music to be used, but Balanchine is satisfied and does not ask for a run-through. It appears he knows basically what he wants, but is not going to be bothered by a precise ending just yet.

"It doesn't matter." He beams with obvious pleasure at his day's work, unperturbed by the inexact ending. The conclusion was already within him.

Pausing a few paces from the rear door, Rouben Ter-Arutunian stands with his feet together until Balanchine beckons him to a chair next to his own. The slight Armenian scenic and costume designer moves with long strides. He is theatrically dressed in tight black pants and shirt with a four-inch-wide brass-studded belt looped around his hips. He settles down next to Balanchine. Despite the fact they have worked together for twenty-six years they maintain a formal distance. Ironically, it is space that bonds them. Balanchine brings life to space and Ter-Arutunian brings space to that life. Today, however, Ter-Arutunian is here to provide costumes. The company's cofounder and general director, Lincoln Kirstein compared Ter-Arutunian's role to Leon Bakst's with Diaghilev's Ballet Russe.

Ter-Arutunian hoped that he would be using the designs from the original *Mozartiana* for the new version. They had been created by the great designer Christian Bérard, who had been a teacher of Ter-Arutunian's at the L'École des Beaux Arts in Paris after the Second World War.

"Okay, now, let us do whole thing from beginning," Balanchine announces. "We have to see how much time it takes." He imitates an officious opera director, and squints at the clock, waiting for the second hand to point to twelve. "Und," he grunts, giving Boelzner an exaggerated downbeat. Andersen and Farrell start their entrance and elegantly parade to the center and continue on, passing and presenting as they remember Balanchine's designs. The ballet master watches, almost shyly, not wanting to stare too hard at his dancers. Ter-Arutunian concentrates, seeing for the first time a ballet that he will have to costume. To be unobtrusive he tucks in his chin, but this innocent gesture only arches his muscular neck. With his dark eyes staring from under his heavy peaked eyebrows, he looks extremely menacing, though every dancer soon learns he is not.

A few dancers watch near the front door. Something has come over Farrell. She is no longer working; she is dancing, attacking the choreography fearlessly—when she goes off balance or out of control she adds embellishments, extra turns off pointe, or new arm movements. She is free enough to trust herself, for she has Balanchine's faith in her.

The first time one runs through a variation, or especially a series of dances, there can be many surprises that are not previously sensed when dancing it in bits and pieces. The most obvious problems arise in pace and phrasing, but sometimes a difficult step that was troublesome at first is less difficult than another that at first presented no problem. Sometimes, simply the placement of a step in the sequence is a shock—because at that moment one may have less breath than expected, or the legs or feet may not have their usual strength after being drained by the preceding dancing.

Balanchine watches the continuity of the musical theme and the development of its variations. Ter-Arutunian smiles. All the stops, starts and sweat have disappeared. Farrell's second variation is over in a moment, with all the trouble she had learning the last intricate combination invisible. Andersen's *pirouettes* are flawless; they produce murmurs from the dancers who have just arrived. Farrell turns too fast, but swivels slowly around on a flat foot in the opening sequence of the fifth variation, giving a remarkable effect of incongruous delicacy. If anyone else had done it, it would look like a clumsy blunder. Their two last variations evolve beautifully, although they are both panting for breath at the finish. But, of course, they have just discovered where they might find places to catch their breath within the newest sequence.

As the other dancers applaud, Farrell looks to Balanchine for an idea for the end of her last variation. He approaches her, smiling, shakes his head, letting her know that there will be something.

"Good. Thank you," he announces, dismissing his dancers. He turns to Ter-Arutunian. Dunleavy quickly gets to Balanchine before he starts discussing costumes with the designer, and asks when the best hours for rehearsal would be tomorrow. After giving the information, Balanchine quickly returns to the designer. He makes flowery gestures along one arm and clamps his wrist and drums four fingers on the top. Undoubtedly he is talking about Andersen's costume, for Balanchine would not want sleeves to cover Farrell's lovely arms. Perhaps Andersen would wear billowy sleeves with a tight cuff of four buttons. The two men leave the studio engrossed in their plans. The next rehearsal begins. Balanchine has not even checked the time of the theme and seven variations, as he has planned to do. In the past three days, six hours of work have been molded into just over five minutes of performance time.

VARIATIONS
VIII AND IX

Balanchine is teaching for the third day in a row, a sign of prolonged interest, and not just whim, as in seasons past. The company senses this, and rejoices, although their bodies are aching from his quixotic demands.

The first rehearsal of *Mozartiana* is ideally set for fifteen minutes after class. During that time, Balanchine talks with Ter-Arutunian in Horgan's office; Andersen, who has danced the demanding role of Apollo the night before, relaxes on the floor, and in a corner Farrell coaches the young Darci Kistler in her own role in the finale of Georges Bizet's *Symphony in C*, while two female soloists stare intently from a discreet distance. Just as the older ballerina is passing on knowledge, a father, Jacques d'Amboise, is giving advice to his son Christopher. When Balanchine enters to start *Mozartiana*, the two men are working on the best angles to present the steps within certain combinations.

The studio clears. Balanchine sits in a metal folding chair. Moredock is ready. Andersen and Farrell walk to the center of the studio and look to their ballet master. Dunleavy has entered and squeaked to a halt. Leland is near the piano with her yellow pad full of recorded steps and corresponding floor patterns. There is more organization today; it is closer to the usual efficiency of things. Maybe Balanchine is more relaxed, confident; maybe the dancers are. The room is electric with the spring of May. The air is clear.

"Just walk through it," says Balanchine, and leans back against the barre. The music comes and the dancers go, reviewing everything they have learned. Soon they dance crisply, instead of walking. When steps are small, one is almost forced to dance them "full out," or else they cannot be seen. Momentum develops. Balanchine asks his dancers only to walk it. But no matter what, his presence makes the dancers want to give everything. Balanchine exudes such innocence and purity that it feels terrible to disappoint him.

Balanchine once again asks them to "mark" it. He is not testing character, to see if one will instead give his all and dance full out. Balanchine actually means it, as he means everything he says, even when his eyes sparkle with whimsy. He is the most direct and honest of artists without ever appearing to be troubled by self-doubt.

Andersen and Farrell finish dancing and Balanchine asks his ballerina if she is tired.

"I was tired before I got here," Farrell says wryly. Balanchine laughs with one of the few people with whom he always has fun. Class was hard and she had danced his flamboyant *Walspurgesnacht Ballet* from Gounod's *Faust* the night before. They banter more. He basks in her wit, beauty and ease. After a few minutes, he forces himself to ask again if she is tired. "I am, but I won't be," she answers now as a disciplined dancer.

The last few bars of Farrell's variation are still not choreographed. Moredock is asked to play them, and continues into the first few measures of the eighth variation. Balanchine is not bothered about the first few measures; instead he concentrates on the new music. Farrell stands where she is. She hasn't been dismissed yet. But her focus on Balanchine is not so strong—it's Andersen's turn to dance.

While searching for an idea, Balanchine takes Farrell's hand. He leads her a few steps to the right, and demonstrates two steps backward on pointe to a *plié* into *arabesque*. She responds, but looks a little disturbed. The combination will take longer than the remaining music at the end of her variation.

"You take his hand," says Balanchine. Only Farrell knows that the eighth variation will not follow the same structure of the previous seven. At least it will be shared with Andersen and quite possibly not be as strenuous as a solo. It will probably be a duet. No wonder Balanchine did not want to finish the variation yesterday. Only then did he realize that he wanted her to have the last solo of the group.

Andersen holds her hand. The two dancers wait. Balanchine places himself in front of Farrell. She knows whatever he does now is meant for her. He repeats the step, but starts on the other foot. She mimics him, moving with his exact timing, in the tempo of the music playing in his mind. Then facing her and holding her hand, Balanchine moves in the direction he wants Andersen to step. The dancer follows behind him, also facing Farrell. High on pointe, the ballerina looks like a movie queen with two suitors pursuing her. Andersen's step is in subtle contrast to hers—he steps with crossed legs to her open legs. Balanchine has placed them on the same feet but faces them toward each other. From a distance it would give the illusion of the opposite.

The ballet master steps away and Andersen takes Farrell's hand. The dancers repeat without the music, completing two sets in both directions before Balanchine stops them. When the staccato music comes it matches her sharp steps on pointe. Farrell and Moredock look at Balanchine for any sign

photo: Costas

1A&B
George Balanchine demonstrating steps.

photo: © Dominique Nabokc

2 George Balanchine upstairs at the Russian Tea Room on February 9, 1981, announc
ing that the New York City Ballet would present a festival to honor Tschaikovsk
in June, 1981.

3A
Roman Jasinsky and Tamara
Toumanova dancing in Balanchine's first *Mozartiana*. It
was presented by Les Ballets
1933, a company Balanchine
formed with Boris Kochno,
and had its premiere June 7,
1933 at the Theatre des
Champs-Elysees in Paris, and
was performed later that year
in London.

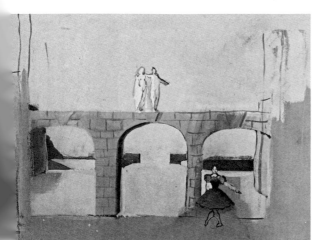

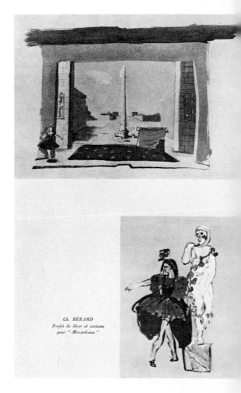

B The set design by Christian Berard for the
original 1933 *Mozartiana*.

3C
Christian Berard's 1945 designs for set and costumes.
The ballet was danced in stylized 18th century
costumes before a set that represented
an Italian town.

Ch. BÉRARD
Projet de décor et costume
pour " Mozartiana "

4A
Charles Laskey and
Holly Howard in the
1934 version of
Mozartiana, per-
formed by the School
of American Ballet
Production Company.

4B In the 1935 American *Mozartiana* Balanchine
had three dancers perform the *gigue*. They
were, left to right, Jack Potteiger, Hortense
Karklyn and Joseph Levinoff.

4C
Frederick Franklin and Alexandra Danilova were the
leading couple in Balanchine's third *Mozartiana*, performed in 1945 by the Ballet Russes de Monte Carlo.

5A&B
Scenes from the original 1933 *Mozartiana*. The *menuet* was performed by six women. Balanchine reduced their number to four in the final 1981 ballet.

photos courtesy of the
Dance Collection
The New York Public
  Library at Lincoln Center
Astor, Lenox and Tilden
  Foundations

5C
A pose from the 1936 *Mozartiana*, performed by The American Ballet. Standing, left to right, Rabana Hasburg, Daphne Vane, Heide Vossler; sitting, left to right, Hortense Karklyn, Helen Leitch.

photo: Costas

6A&B   Balanchine in rehearsal of *Mozartiana*, May, 1981. Peter Martins stands at the barre.

photo: Costas

7*A* In the Main Rehearsal Hall, Balanchine works out steps to fill the last twelve bars of music for the *pas de deux* in *Mozartiana* with Suzanne Farrell. Jerri Kumery, one of the four dancers in the *menuet*, sits against the wall in angel wings designed for the ballet *Le Pathetique*, also presented at the Tschaikovsky Festival.

7*B* Front line, left to right: Dara Adler, Suzanne Farrell, Ib Andersen, Lisa Cantor, dancing what came to be called "the trouble step" in the finale of *Mozartiana*.

8   Suzanne Farrell and Ib Andersen in the final pose of the *pas de deux*.

to stop. He approaches his couple without any directorial sign, such as the clap of John Taras' hands, or the short whistles of Jerome Robbins. A dancer rarely felt he was being directed by Balanchine, only led or persuaded.

Andersen has been starting on the wrong foot more often than not, and is corrected by Balanchine who gently suggests that they continue the same combination, but move diagonally downstage left. Andersen adroitly moves backward toward the center of the room.

On the third set, the dancers follow him back across the center and around in a circle. Essentially, the same combination of steps has been subtly changed simply by presenting it to the audience in a variety of angles. Farrell's legs extend in the air what Andersen's do on the floor, making a variation within the combination. The step is easy after their killing variation, and yet they still fill the space, building with the same pattern as the music.

Watching it repeated, one understands one of the distinguishing characteristics of Balanchine's work—he makes you see the music. Balanchine does it so unobtrusively that one hardly realizes why he feels so completely comfortable watching and listening. Balanchine adds a kick for Andersen.

They continue and Andersen, pivoting Farrell in place on her right leg, leads her around again in a circle under his arm, encircling the ballerina as though she were a gift being wrapped. The step Andersen does around her does not lend much support but she retains her line and élan.

Balanchine builds. He asks his dancers to expand into circles around themselves, finally separating and circling the stage to stand apart, facing front. Andersen is asked to face Farrell. It is a common and powerful statement of Balanchine's: the man and woman face the world—separate but joined.

Andersen is allowed no closer. Farrell gazes at the imaginary audience. Maybe this is what Balanchine was referring to when he told Boelzner the other day about a dance being like a conversation. Probably Andersen will move first, since Farrell will have been dancing for quite a time.

"Going on," Balanchine cues, and Moredock plays the next phrase of music; it sounds totally unrelated to anything heard before.

The dancers wait for Balanchine but he runs past them in tiny steps on the balls of his feet, with his arms down near his body. He flexes his wrists, palms parallel to the floor. He is the picture of a ballet girl scooting onto the stage and circling the posing dancers in what Jerome Robbins calls "piddle steps." Balanchine is the most bashful little girl one ever saw. After blushing on cue, he smiles more broadly than anyone else. The music stops and Dunleavy and Leland follow. Rejuvenated they squeak and clomp, making horrified faces and wisecracks—wondering how they are going to remember this slapdash presentation. Balanchine is hurriedly inventing with three bodies where eventually four will intertwine in overlapping patterns.

The scene is reminiscent of the mesmerized children dressed as insects in the mysterious forest kingdom of Oberon and Titania in Balanchine's ballet of Mendelssohn's *A Midsummer Night's Dream.* Presumably the four lucky girls who dance in *Mozartiana* will be the four little girls who were presented to Balanchine in costume two days before.

Deni Lamont comes in and watches. He was one of the finest dancers in the Ballets Russes' last years, before he joined the New York City Ballet twenty-one years ago and became a soloist. Still in shape, he now dances Indian ritual dances in performance, and works as a liaison among all factions of the company—dancers, musicians and administration.

Balanchine tells Andersen and Farrell, along with everyone else, to *chaînée* off to the sides of the studio, and quite possibly off the stage. They spin toward their appointed corners.

Moredock plays the music, but they have all reached the walls while the cadenza of the music continues. The notes spiral down as Moredock leans farther and farther to his left. Leland rebounds off the wall to continue spinning, and giggles at the prolonged length of the cadenza. Smiling, Balanchine leaves his chair and looks over Moredock's shoulder and spots his miscalculation.

The pianist plays again. The master solves the problem by starting Andersen and Farrell four beats later than the imaginary girls, and, still turning, has them circle back to the center by the end of the cadenza. The spacing and timing work out perfectly, but Balanchine decides it would be better if, after spinning out to the sides, they run back to each other. It cuts out the tricky maneuver of turning back on oneself, and it also looks more passionate.

Moredock begins the start of the ninth variation. Balanchine burlesques playing the violin, as though he is wearing a mop wig. Leland and Farrell play-act a schmaltzy *grand pas de deux*. In the pause, Lamont talks to Dunleavy in a stage whisper.

"See if Gordon is ready," she asks him. When he returns he announces, "The orchestra rehearsal isn't finished yet, but they will arrive shortly." After the brief interlude and another recital, they begin with alacrity. "This will only be approximate," Balanchine says. "The piano can't play like a violin and on the solos I want to let the violin be free . . . and play however it wants."

He has Moredock play the new measures, and with great verve mimes the part the violin plays. The dancers listen closely. Prepared for what is to come musically, Balanchine approaches them. Facing Farrell, he lifts his hand high over his head and to the side of the ballerina.

"*Developpé*," he says. She rises onto pointe and unfolds her leg to the desired height with the smoothness of a swan stretching its neck. Andersen supports her with the conventional hold, of both hands on either side of her waist, but Balanchine asks him instead to maintain her balance by holding her wrists with her arms extended to the side.

Balanchine stands with his back to Andersen imitating her. His arms are held akimbo from the shoulder. At the point of the violin's first appearance in this variation, he whips around once, finishing with his leg behind him. Farrell swings her right leg, from high above her ear, and, using its momentum and weight, lets it drop and swing as she swivels and finishes with her leg high behind her while bending her supporting leg to the desired position. Andersen instinctively supports her around the waist as she turns. After another attempt and a correction to Farrell for leaning forward too much in *arabesque*, Balanchine lunges to his left and assumes the position he would like Andersen to maintain while keeping Farrell on balance. It is an unconventional pose. The partner must move in the opposite direction of the ballerina's momentum.

Balanchine shows Andersen again and again. The dancer doesn't look quite right. Like most classical male dancers, while partnering he likes to point his feet and turn out his legs. It maintains the look and line one has when dancing alone. However, Balanchine does not care about these finer points; he wants something else. Andersen and Farrell eventually master the step after repeated demonstrations by Balanchine, in thick-soled street shoes moving more gracefully than the ballet dancers. He snaps and finishes softly with the violin phrase.

"Try finishing like this," Balanchine suggests to Andersen as he supports Farrell by pressing his wrist against her waist instead of grasping her with his hand. Instantly, it lends an air of foppishness. Balanchine's large hand emerges from the cuff on his Western shirt. Andersen positions himself. Balanchine nods approvingly at the interesting detail. But when Farrell turns into this position, Andersen has much less control of her. It is like trying to catch something falling away from you with your wrist, as you lean in the opposite direction. She adjusts to this by not turning quite so fast.

Boelzner arrives with apologies for being late, and, shortly after, the front door swings open again. "Reporting for duty, sir." It is the concertmaster of the ballet orchestra, Lamar Alsop. He enters, violin and bow tucked under his arm, holding a music stand.

Balanchine escorts this friendly saxophone-playing violinist to Boelzner and lets them play for a while, in much the same way as he lets his dancers dance until there is something wrong. He has said to dancers, "God put me here on earth to tell you what is wrong about you. You have friends to tell you what is good."

The timbre of the violin is lush. "Good," says Balanchine. Alsop stops and excuses his playing. "I just found out two days ago we were doing this. How much of it is being done?" It's a good question, since all choreographers use bits and pieces of complete musical scores. John Taras used the same theme and variations for his Marquis de Cuevas production of *Tarasiana* in 1951.

"We use all of it, naturally," replies Balanchine. The violinist is cued to play again.

"How do you want it?"

"However you want it."

Alsop has realized he has just made an error—many musicians feel they have to adapt to the dancers' usual inability to dance to the music's true tempo. But Balanchine never has had the musicians play along with the dancers; he has trained them to dance to the musicians.

"Slower?" Alsop asks as he starts playing again. "Faster?"

"No matter," says Balanchine, looking at the clock and signaling his dancers to synchronize. But Alsop is too cautious, for the speed of the whipping turn is laboriously mastered.

Instantly, Balanchine springs into a frenzied Paganini imitation, showing Alsop how he wishes him to play as clearly as if he were showing a dancer to dance. The violinist becomes freer. In his brief solo, Alsop phrases in such a way as to effect a quality of unevenness—reproducing exactly the accentuation that Balanchine has demonstrated. He smiles, for now the dancers' precarious swivels are as daring as the violin's phrasings.

The hour and fifteen minutes are gone and everyone listens to the musicians play the ninth variation to the end. "When you have time, go over it; come and play for me," Balanchine suggests to Boelzner and Alsop, "and we will make a cassette tape in my room downstairs."

"How about Tuesday?" the violinist replies. "Maybe even Sunday."

Balanchine nods vigorously at this show of enthusiasm, apparently innocent of the fact that everyone in his company tried to give him as much as he gave them of himself.

VARIATION IX
ON THE THEME

———————— ⚬⚭ ————————

Farrell stands at the barre warming up the following Sunday morning. She is in full stage makeup—false lashes shelter blue eyes lined and shadowed with added color appropriate to the lights in *Vienna Waltzes*, the ballet she will dance at the matinee. The mood of the piece matches the purple blue around her eyes. Her pale skin is paler with powder and her hair is brushed, folded and sparkling with rhinestones.

Other dancers also have their makeup on in varying stages —only one eye finished, or base color and facial shading with no eyes or blocked-out eyebrows. Weekend classes always carry a carnival air, since they are followed by less-pressured matinees, instead of the usual full day of rehearsals before an evening performance.

The master of ceremonies arrives. After the barre, Balanchine expresses his disapproval with the way one of the girls holds her hands. A lecture ensues.

"The hands are dead!" he says, holding his arms to the side but letting his hands droop from the wrists imitating the position he didn't like—something he always said looked like the feet of a dead chicken.

"They can't be stiff like this, either," he says, tightening them and holding his fingers straight as if they were glued together like "puppet hands." "They have to be alive!" he continues, methodically prying each finger apart. "Hands have fingers and fingers are not dead either." As he begins to wiggle them, he brings the back of his hand to his nose and peers at the girl slowly waving his fingers. "They reach, have life. Like tentacles they go past, they see like . . . THEM!"

A few of the dancers burst out laughing, especially Judy Fugate. The reason is she knows what he is referring to; it is *Them*, a movie on television the previous night about giant killer ants that invade Los Angeles. With his fingers he is imitating their antennae. Balanchine's taste ran to science fiction and astronomy; but he also loved quiz shows, *Wonder Woman* and *Charlie's Angels*. Home for Balanchine meant rest and resting the mind allowed for greater concentration later. He did not have a stereo or piano in his apartment, only a radio. He would listen to WQXR in the mornings, often while ironing, before he went to the theater. The theater and his room in it—with a piano—were where he worked.

Just before the start of the *Mozartiana* rehearsal, Balanchine speaks of something more sophisticated than what he has alluded to in class. Boelzner's musical entrance prompts a discussion of the relationship between the composer and the musical score. Farrell says to Balanchine, "I know you won't, because I'm telling you to, but you should see *Amadeus*. I saw it recently and it was really—"

"No," Balanchine interrupts. "And I'm not going to."

"See?" Farrell says mischievously to Boelzner, who had just heard her complete review of the Broadway play.

"It's awful and shameful, the way they show Mozart," Balanchine continues. "It's not true. They have taken this from a poem by Pushkin! It is called 'Amadeus.' I recited it when I was little boy in school in Russia. This poem that Pushkin wrote was written for fun. Pushkin was not serious, even though it was very beautiful at the end. I remember."

"Well, at least for the production, the sets and costumes," Farrell says with a smaller voice.

"What about Rimsky-Korsakov's opera about Mozart? Wonderful music. They should do that! Why doesn't anybody do that?" Balanchine asks, facing Boelzner. "He will be sorry in heaven."

The door opens and the photographer Costas enters. Balanchine asked him as a friend, not as a photographer, to the rehearsal. He carries a present rather than a camera—a large tin of French cookies, which Balanchine accepts with a bow and thanks in Greek.

It is time to work now though, not to eat. "You won't want to do the whole thing today, do you?" Balanchine asks Andersen and Farrell. He wants to start where he left off two days ago. The dancers seem relieved, though they don't expect to review the whole ballet in this easy Sunday atmosphere. This week both of them have performed ten ballets.

Balanchine starts to forge ahead but soon looks genuinely bewildered, standing motionless as the second hand circles the clock for minutes.

"Do from beginning." The dancers start from the beginning of the *pas de deux*. Calmly, Boelzner plays the two orchestral phrases and one violin break, then stops at the exact note. It sounds like time for another violin break. Hesitating only briefly, and with a clearer idea of the dance's continuity, the ballet master turns away from Farrell and dashes off to his right before coming back to her and lunging deeply. Andersen jumps in the same direction, and Balanchine says, "*Chaîné*," before he returns to Farrell. Andersen responds by spinning back to his partner and lunging before her. The music ended too soon. Balanchine has Andersen repeat, starting a bit sooner and finishing on time. But the lunge is not low enough. The sequence is difficult, for Andersen has to support Farrell behind him upon his immediate return.

"Am I on pointe?" she asks Balanchine.

"No," he says. This is easier for both dancers to control. They do it again, but Andersen comes up from the lunge too soon, in an attempt to facilitate his support of his partner.

"Lower, lowyer, lawyer," Balanchine says, using a favorite quip. The dancers work on the sequence for a few minutes until they coordinate with the music and are sure of each other's balance.

Judging from the music heard two days ago, difficulties loom throughout this *pas de deux*. The violin forays continue throughout the whole dance, and Balanchine is asking for stops as abrupt as each of the violin's. The timing is going to have to be rehearsed repeatedly to achieve complete co-ordination with an orchestra. A dancer can usually sense how each conductor will take the music, just as a good ballet con-ductor is aware of particular tendencies and limitations of dancers' techniques. If there is confusion a dancer can always search for the downbeat. But with Balanchine clearly giving freedom to the violin, each break is bound to be different. All will have to be extremely sensitive to the subtlety of the vari-ous tempos which could transform the most beautifully ex-ecuted combination into a clumsy or unclear finish—a chal-lenging prospect for the dancer.

Balanchine appears unconcerned by these possibilities, as he steps to his left foot, moving his right foot behind him, then twisting in place before facing Farrell while holding his head tilted slightly sideways. She continues this outward spinning step, a *piqué pirouette en dehors en croisé ara-besque*. Balanchine first used it in *Don Quixote*, and he knows it has a look on her unmatched by any other ballerina.

"Don't do on time," he instructs. She stops and Boelzner begins once more. "Not on time. Just go," Balanchine says. For emphasis he shoves his hands away from himself. It works. Although his request sounds unmusical, the dancing looks lighter and easier and gives more lift to the music.

Leland enters resplendent in satin pumps, her hair piled high in a Napoleonic bouffant hairdo.

"Going on," he says, showing Farrell while having Andersen continue in the opposite direction. They circle the stage and spin to each other, then cross one another, stepping into *arabesques*. Balanchine often achieves accentuation by freezing blocks of cross movement; as now by precisely setting the picture he wants with the raised legs, extended arms, and arched backs. For a moment he looks at this shape before the dancers flow into the next *arabesque*.

After more combinations toward center, Farrell is now stepping like an egret in a marsh, probably only wishing the floor felt so soft. "Two jumps back," Balanchine says, beginning to lift Farrell off the floor as she starts to respond. But she pushes down on his wrists and they walk backward in tandem, rather than with Balanchine continuing to lift her in the air as he would have done a few years ago. Then a ballerina would have jumped as much as possible to seem lighter. But Farrell and Balanchine have nothing to prove to each other. She looks touched by his enthusiasm.

Andersen steps in and lifts Farrell, but not as abruptly as the music demands. He tries again. He is less muscular than most men in the company, and Farrell, at five feet seven inches and as lean as ever, is still not a small woman. This *pas de deux* is the first time these two have been paired, and these are their first lifts.

"Bang!" yells Balanchine, clapping his hands and stamping his foot simultaneously before smiling, "that's how I want it. That's what should be." Andersen lifts Farrell again.

"Thaaat's right." The next attempt gets a "good." Farrell smiles over her shoulder at her sweating partner. Balanchine is already stepping toward the corner to demonstrate the next combination. After learning this preparatory circle of high steps around herself, Farrell and Andersen circle smoothly together, with Farrell being lifted like a horse on a carousel, rising at intervals, perfectly timed with the musical accents.

"No. No," says the choreographer, stepping in Andersen's place. "She jumps *to* you.'" He stands ahead of Farrell and motions for her to come. She jumps to him and he catches her for a second before letting her down. He scoots a few paces ahead for her next jump and repeats around the circle for the third and last time. This is in keeping with the dance so far— a *pas de deux*, where, instead of the two bodies moving as one and rarely letting go of each other, they dance together and yet separately, with one following the other or breaking apart, or starting without the other, only to finish at peaks while keeping their rapport as one. It matches the chase of violin against orchestra—a feeling of an elusive love. The dance has poignancy in its playfulness. Balanchine's ballets are often criticized for being emotionless or cold, yet they give the spectator room for his own connotations, space for his imagination to roam. All of them give a new perspective on how men and women are together. In response to a critic, Balanchine said, "When you say we have no soul, it merely means our soul is unlike yours."

The dancers have much more difficulty with this new version. The step-in, step-away is very difficult for the man, especially if he wants to look graceful as he achieves the desired effect.

After a few minutes, struggling to keep two circles parallel without touching and sensing when his partner would jump, Andersen is forced to break some of his former partnering habits. The problems eventually work out because he has stretched his technique. However, it is hard to dance this sequence on time. After many attempts, the carousel ride is transformed into the scene of a circus trainer with his horse jumping through a hoop. It is as daring as the music is becoming.

With Farrell having flown into Andersen's hands three

times, Balanchine now has her spin away from him. The way Boelzner's fingers run up the keyboard, one can tell there is another violin break. Farrell ends in *arabesque* and Andersen rushes to stop her and help her hold her balance by taking her wrists as she bows her back.

"Bam!" Balanchine says at the abrupt stop and facile curve.

He holds Farrell's wrists, moves behind her, switching places with Andersen and then flies away. She holds her balance, comes off pointe and watches Balanchine, already ten feet away, amazingly spin and finish facing her. Immediately he signals her to turn. She pirouettes and he runs back, catching her before she finishes off pointe. Farrell's face is full of surprise; she expected to finish on her own. Andersen just stands staring.

"What would you like to do?" Balanchine asks, grinning at Andersen, who is still awed by the choreographer's performance. "When you leave her. You know something?" Balanchine lifts his arm into the air and vaguely outlines a virtuoso something. Andersen realizes the step should cover the same space on the floor as in the music—ten feet forward and back in eight counts.

"A double *assemblé* into *pirouettes*," suggests the dancer, having translated Balanchine's twirling hand.

"Good."

Andersen demonstrates the twisting, angled leap and lands with his feet perfectly together before stepping into a double *pirouette* and dashing back to Farrell. He arrives late. Balanchine suggests landing from the jump on only one foot, allowing him to step immediately and turn. Time and momentum are also saved. Andersen attempts the rarely danced double *sauté de basque en tournant en passé arrière* into his double *pirouette*, before catching Farrell. He is late again, though the step is no longer awkward for she turns an extra time to compensate. Balanchine is not fooled. Nor is he satisfied until there is no need for compromise.

"Good. I think that is all for today," Balanchine says finally. "But maybe, from the beginning." It is understood that he means the beginning of the *pas de deux*.

Through five forays of the imaginary violin, Boelzner plays the part of the orchestra. Costas is smiling. The variation is done. At the conclusion, Balanchine walks to the piano and offers the cookies to his dancers.

"Are they butter?" asks the Danish dancer.

"Naturlich," replies Balanchine, who on the company free day tomorrow will receive the Austrian Decoration of Honor for Science and Art.

VARIATION IX, CONTINUED

———————— ?◆ ————————

Balanchine starts his second week of teaching at his usual incredible pace. While the dancers feel for signs of possible improvement within their bodies, he tours the barre searching for lack of development. Some are corrected and sent toward new horizons within their technique. Finally a melody breaks the intensity.

"That was Josephine Baker. Yes?" he asks de Soto at the piano. "Yes. I think it's 'Petite Josephine,' " says the lanky pianist.

"When I was in France . . . a hundred years ago," begins Balanchine, "she invited me over to help her cook. There was to be a big party. I got there and she opened the door of her Paris apartment. She was stark naked . . . and white! I looked. She welcomed me in . . . very gracious. She was covered with flour, top to bottom. Making bread, she was. She was famous for baking bread."

Before Balanchine continues class he turns to de Soto. "She had beautiful long legs . . . beautiful."

In the center Balanchine gives *bourrées*; reams of *bourrées*, forward, backward, in circles. The girls wave back and forth across the room with their feet hitting the floor at two hundred beats a minute. Over the years many of his classes concentrated on only one step. Whether they were soft landings from jumps, or stretched and far-reaching awareness of body line in strengthening adagio work, or brilliant footwork and extremely important preparatory steps, all were performed to a multitude of rhythms. Today it is *bourrées*.

"Boys too. It is good for boys."

He is right. So often men dance big, virtuoso steps but cannot move lightly over the floor, or they are sloppy when they do. Ideally, Balanchine does not believe boys or men should be taught by women; all the men's classes at the School of American Ballet are taught by men. However, he often said men should dance like women, meaning they should have enough versatility to be able to lift their legs as high, move their feet as quickly, and have as supple a body, while at the same time maintaining and presenting masculine grace from within. Yet when women dance traditional men's steps that require athletic prowess—great twisting leaps, multiple beats of the legs or spinning—they look like athletes and are not beautiful in the classical sense.

By the time Balanchine reenters the Main Hall for *Mozartiana*, Andersen has caught his breath from his rehearsal of *A Midsummer Night's Dream*, which required his feet to move as quickly as *bourrées* but in the air. Balanchine bows quickly to his dancers and the pianist, anxious to make up for the lost time over the weekend. He worked only an hour on Sunday, and lost more time on Monday, the company's free day. Union rules that limit rehearsal time on weekends, due to the heavy performance schedule and the inviolate free day, place enough restrictions on the management to make all choreographers feel as though there is rarely enough time allowed to develop their ballets.

"Let's see what we have," Balanchine says, and grabs a chair. Andersen changes his drenched shirt. He has five more hours of rehearsal and two ballets tonight. Farrell is in place.

The music and dancers progress until the steps end abruptly at the unfilled time.

"Maybe you should come off pointe," he says, going back and referring to the second step in the *pas de deux*; the only sequence worked on, time and again with the violinist four days ago. Farrell executes the fast swivel with Andersen's support, and now finishes off pointe as he lunges. The step looks more secure. With the added confidence that the change gives to the ballerina, the step now has as surprising an effect as the first entrance of the violin.

Balanchine turns to his right and swings his right leg at knee level. He whistles to emphasize the strong accent of each kick before it trails off. Without words, expletive sounds of whooshes, chirps and bams express the essence of what he wants in the steps. He stands back and watches Farrell spin and fan her leg in a high arch over her head.

Balanchine wrinkles his nose at his new combination and decides upon less complicated turns *en attitude*, with the back leg bent at a right angle. Farrell looks at him sideways.

"You know I don't like *attitudes*," she says, feigning the distress of an old-fashioned Russian prima ballerina. Balanchine only smiles. She sails around in a few turns. Farrell rarely dances *en attitude* on stage. for she looks magnificent extending the truncated *attitude* into the long straight line of *arabesque*. Balanchine eventually reverts to the fan kicks—a rare moment of return in his "hundred years" of assembling ballets.

Balanchine continues to work with Farrell as Andersen uses Leland as a surrogate partner, before switching back to Farrell—when Balanchine is decided on what follows. After the pianist plays a break of the imaginary violin, sending Farrell off hopping with *ballottés* and quick *passés*, Balanchine has Andersen catch her by the hand. She stops, caught on pointe with one foot held at the side of her knee.

"Go away," the ballet master says, holding her hand and

pointing to her hip. She juts her hip out in the opposite direction from him, causing her body to bend off balance to his resistance. It lends a sexy, jazzy flavor, and exaggerates the line from the formal. He steps close to her, one foot pointed on the floor ahead of him, and they bend slightly at the waist in a *révérence* as elegant as anything seen in the court of Louis XVI.

Andersen watches her dance and rushes in.

"Too early. Let her fall." Again Balanchine takes her hand and tells her to bend away as if they were in a tug of war.

"Use other hand," Balanchine suggests. "I'm sorry, I can't show with this hand. Last night I was getting in a car and bang, someone sat on it. I can't hold anything today." He examines his limp paw. He had not choreographed difficult hand switches or strenuous lifts. Most of the dancing only entailed brief partnering. Generally choreographers make combinations similar to the natural movement of their own bodies. The limitations of their own bodies' kinetic habits are more evident in new choreographers, but is sometimes more easily detected in great ones when they are injured.

For years when Balanchine had a bad knee, he inevitably asked his dancers to kneel on the same knee. He had to consciously rethink the step if he wanted the other knee; and if he leapt, the jump would naturally land on his strong leg. A dancer usually discovered what had happened the next day, when he tried to figure out why just one leg was sore and not the other. Everything that had required strength was on Balanchine's leg with the good knee.

Boelzner plays the next musical phrase. "It is like old man walking," Balanchine says, slowly approaching Andersen. But what he asks is far from what he says. Balanchine sends the Dane off into a high twirling leap toward the back corner upstage, before leading Farrell to the center in a combination which ends in a slow half turn *en arabesque*. Balanchine scoots over to Andersen and has him continue into a larger version of his brush step from his first variation, before having them turn alternately facing each other two feet apart. The dancers are reduced to a fit of giggles as they see each other's turning faces at such close range. Balanchine is anxious to continue.

"Music, please."

But the dancers do not finish on time until Balanchine has them overlap one another's finish. He continues with a tricky *promenade*, quickly devised but very hard to execute. Farrell excuses herself to put on new toe shoes for better support. With the added support from the new shoes, Farrell gets a more secure and less painful pivot than with the older and softer shoes.

"This upcoming bit is a little weird," Boelzner says, before playing a dissonant passage. Balanchine knows it is there, and walks over to read the incongruous bit of music.

"Tchaikovsky brought Mozart up to date . . . and if Mozart had lived he probably would have turned into Stravinsky," Balanchine says matter-of-factly. Boelzner nods in agreement. "He was a genius, a true genius," Balanchine continues. "You know, when he was trying to get into the conservatory, in London, I think, where Handel and Bach went—you know, they didn't let him in. They said he was too young. He was baby," says Balanchine placing his hand at knee level. "The people in the conservatory said he would have to listen to some music and write down what he could remember. They said, 'We have all done this test, which of course they hadn't, and they made him listen to some awful music for two hours —two hours—and he returned to them, every note written perfectly. Everyone bowed to this boy and let him in. . . . Now that's a genius!" he concludes, punctuating the air with his finger.

Balanchine walks to the center deep in thought. The dancers return to the still figure. Then as if to match the composer's surprising atonality, Balanchine asks Farrell to do the most convoluted and difficult combination yet crafted for the ballet. He whirls around, throws his leg back, bends over and immediately swings himself up, steps onto the other foot and finishes with a "bang." The two dancers and Leland stand dumfounded. Slowly the ballet master goes over it, directing Andersen when exactly to step in and catch Farrell's arm behind her back at the same speed of her turn so not to break the impetus for the next turn. This she will dance completely unsupported until she comes out of it and steps forward. The two dancers mark the mechanics of the sequence very slowly. They feel each other's space, timing and balance. Andersen senses when to avoid the swinging leg. Soon Farrell turns a double *pirouette* and continues to bend down with her head to her knee, as her free foot points to the ceiling in a huge circular sweeping movement. Andersen barely touches her. From the swing of her leg she gathers force and goes into a triple *pirouette, plié* off pointe and then a swivel up to a *coupé posé.* Leland's jaw drops.

"Never again," the ballerina says. Anderson is speechless; Balanchine is happy; Boelzner missed it. Next time he watches and she does it again. She giggles at herself and Balanchine smiles and nods.

"Play the last phrase in the music," Balanchine says without fanfare. The dancers look at each other with a mixture of surprise and feigned relief. The music returns to a gentle finish. In the pause, Balanchine is still smiling to himself. He turns and looks at Farrell. "You know the ending in *Symphony in C?*" he asks rhetorically, alluding to his Bizet ballet and the famous finish of the second movement adagio in which Farrell performs so passionately, melting into her partner's arms as he slowly steps backward, until he kneels, with her laying backward and facing up, draped over one knee. "Well, I stole that from *Mozartiana.* I thought I would never have to do *Mozartiana* again," he says, shrugging his shoulders and letting his hands drop to his thighs in an exaggerated sigh. "It was nothing before. Nobody liked it or remembered it," he says of the 1945 version, "so I took this finish I had used for Danilova. It was perfect. But now we need something else."

The dancers take the previous pose from the turns and as the music continues, Balanchine has Andersen kneel; but he can't figure what to do for Farrell. He has always stolen from himself throughout his career but he wanted something new. As the music finishes Farrell wantonly flops onto her partner's knee, into the position she has done so often in *Symphony in C.* Balanchine bursts out laughing.

Robert Irving enters and walks noiselessly to the piano. His large red sneakers are in sharp contrast to his rather formal demeanor, though they do match his warmth and good humor. Balanchine greets the musical director and repeats the explanation he has given Boelzner, of the freedom of the violin.

Andersen and Farrell dance the whole *pas de deux* with speed, abrupt chasing, catching, stepping, separating, joining and intimacy.

At the finish, Balanchine stands and asks Farrell for her best leg in *arabesque.* She lifts the one most comfortable for her.

"Wrong leg."

She hikes up the other. It is still not right. Neither are the next few poses. Balanchine sits down. Boelzner and Irving wait on the piano bench. The dancers switch from one tired foot to another. Leland leans against the barre. There is still a half-hour left to the two-hour rehearsal. Balanchine sits expressionless, for a long time. His chest sinks into his stomach. His hands lie limp in his lap; one consoles the other. The heat of energy is gone. Quietly, in his nasal voice, he mutters, "That is all."

The action on the stage was in sharp contrast to the quiet of the Main Rehearsal Hall. The conceptual designer Kermit

Love is talking with scenic and costume designer Rouben Ter-Arutunian. Love wears an enormous pair of wings that rise eight feet above his head. And his head is circled by a ring of white hair extending from behind his ears to a full beard. His cherubic face looks like Santa Claus; appropriately, for he has brought children such gifts as Big Bird, Snuffle-upagus and Cookie Monster of *Sesame Street*. This inventive man had worked with Balanchine as an assistant stage manager during Balanchine's Broadway days in the late thirties and early forties; he made enlargements of Isamu Noguchi's symbolically sculptural sets to fit the dimensions of the New York State Theater stage and constructed wings for new productions of *The Firebird*. Love had also used his extraordinary puppeteering skills when he designed the forty-foot mace-swinging giant in Balanchine's *Don Quixote*. While working on the phantasmagorical effects for Balanchine's version of Ravel's *L'Enfant et les Sortilèges*, he was asked by Balanchine to enhance Ter-Arutunian's costumes and build wings for angels.

This prompted a rumor that Balanchine was going to choreograph the funereal last movement of Tchaikovsky's final symphony, the *Pathétique*. These wings were for that. Although no one could dance in them, they could be used in a processional.

In his melodic voice, Love does his best to answer Ter-Arutunian's questions—explaining that the bamboo-structured wings can stay bent and maintain an interesting three-dimensional shape when viewed from the front. To see their effect and test their proportions the seven-foot and ten-foot wings are modeled on the stage. It takes a little time to persuade Ter-Arutunian that gouging out designs at different depths would allow varying amounts of light to pass through the wings and thus make these wings far superior to detailed painting.

The men also view and discuss wigs, masks and robes of re-dyed New York City Opera costumes. But not until Balanchine walks onto the stage is anything resolved. Within minutes, his direct decisions as to how to use the colors, textures and proportions, give his coworkers clear images by which to guide themselves.

MENUET

—⚜—

"Awful, awful thing!" Balanchine announces as he flies into the Practice Room the next day. "How could they kill Pope? Pope is like God. The closest man can be to God. . . They are Communists. The K.G.B. They have to be." He tells his dancers that in 1972, on the last company tour to Russia, he heard on Soviet radio a call to support "our comrades in Ireland." Balanchine claims at the time that no one would believe what he had heard. But now, finally, maybe, with the Secretary of State and President claiming that all terrorism in the Western world is backed by the Soviet Union, something might finally be done about what he had known for years. The day Congress chose Alexander Haig, Balanchine celebrated with vodka in his office.

The six dancers called to this rehearsal draw closer to the animated storyteller. Soon his raging calms as the tall girls gaze down at him like sunflowers. News of such magnitude broke through the fragility of this theater world as if it were a child's room.

The stories die down, and after a few teasing references to the women's boyfriends, Balanchine walks to the pianist to prepare a dance for *his* women.

Balanchine takes the hand of Nina Fedorova, the tallest, the most languid and one of the most beautiful women in the company. This creature stands in place obediently. Then he fetches another. Victoria Hall is the newest member among the four chosen for the *menuet* and is the only one in the room who has never worked on a new ballet with Balanchine, but like all of them she has studied at his school. She does not look as tall as the others because her body has more muscle, which gives power to her strong technique. Balanchine places her to the front but outside flaxen-haired Fedorova, before leading Jerri Kumery to her place in the back across from Fedorova. Balanchine smiles briefly at the fine shape Kumery is in after coming back from micro knee surgery. The last woman, Susan Freedman, is already standing in place in front, opposite Hall, by the time Balanchine turns around. This extremely long-legged dancer smiles at him eagerly. He watches the women form a regular trapezoid, and smiles in response. The news of the Pope fades from the studio.

Balanchine stands before Freedman, who is nearest, and raises his right arm, curving it high to frame his head. He bends his body at the waist toward the center of the studio as he dips his right knee and bows. Freedman follows him exactly and crosses her left foot briefly behind her right and quickly hoists herself onto pointe when he steps onto the balls of his moccasined feet. Kumery follows closely behind; while Dunleavy, in the back, and Hall and Fedorova, on the opposite side of the studio, mirror the two steps by starting with their left arms up. Only understudy Garielle Whittle stands up and follows.

After telling Freedman to lower her body in the courteous *révérence*, Balanchine immediately has her take three steps around on pointe while presenting each step with a small curled wrist gesture. He asks Freedman to exaggerate this movement, forcing her to bend her otherwise stiff arms. It is the same arm gesture as Farrell's at the end of the first variation.

Boelzner looks for Balanchine's nod and plays the 3/4-time music as the ballet master watches his dancers, who repeat the same steps, starting in the other direction. After hearing the music once again, Balanchine asks the two girls in the back to start the whole sequence two counts later. Balanchine often uses this cannon effect. It shows the full value of the music and sometimes illuminates the underlying beat which may have been unnoticed.

Balanchine immediately returns to Freedman, adds a little double kick jump and finishes with a twist on one leg. "Jump," he warns, just before Freedman shows that she understands the step. Her long legs kick above his head. Balanchine stops her and asks that she jump more and kick less. She responds. "Now kick and jump," he commands. The others respond to his individual corrections as he makes his rounds.

A repeat of the high-kicking jump is followed by a larger kick and another quick twist, finishing with a deep *révérence*. Fedorova's pliable body unfurls along the full length of her leg in the low bow. "Thaaat's right!" says Balanchine, and points to her, proclaiming to the others that that is how that step should look.

After some adjustments and demonstrations of how steps should be danced, Balanchine leads Dunleavy to the center of the four women. "Man will have done variation. But instead of running off, he will walk down center." Balanchine has Dunleavy fill in for the missing man. The music starts from the beginning and he gestures her slowly forward through the frame of the four dancers. Their rock-hard toe shoes whiz past her ears. The comparatively small assistant scrunches her shoulders and closes her eyes, stepping in as straight a line as possible. Chuckling, Balanchine leads her to the back of the small studio. A picture of a prone body from an earlier production comes to mind.

"That's what I want. Big girls with long legs. Not small girls with big heads," says Balanchine at the completion of the sequence. He demonstrates what they will dance next and has them bow sideways to the departing man—this is a variation on the earlier *révérances*. All the troubles with his back now seem to be gone as he shows the dancers how to lunge deeply. The dancers repeat the movements, they stop, grouped in a square. Continuing, Balanchine walks with the music holding Dunleavy's shoulders as the women dance the phrase they have just learned. He turns her torso slightly at the appropriate time to acknowledge their *révérences* to her. They repeat without his assistance. Balanchine goes on, straightening the square they have formed into a single line by having each woman circle until they come into the correct position. The circling takes quite a few minutes to accomplish but fills only two bars of music. It was amazing how often the simplest movement or design took so long to assemble. The average of most choreographers on a very good day was an hour's work for a minute of music.

"One, two, three, four," says Balanchine, pointing down the line at each bowing woman. "Go up," he says, hopping up in his moccasins. He has the four dancers step, turn and bow to each other. By having them step on pointe away from each other, Balanchine slightly enlarges the square, then spreads it wider with a large jump and spinning *bourrées* to the corners. At the same time Fedorova and Freedman leap past each other at mid-stage. Fedorova splits her legs in a perfect one hundred eighty degrees with this chance to move at fullest capacity. For a moment, the onlookers are humbled by her expansive beauty and unleashed talent.

Working methodically, only four beats at a stretch, Balanchine teaches the quartet the next combination. He works with them on the execution of the steps. It is something he did not have to do with Farrell. He asks Kumery to present her feet more precisely and Freedman to give her extensions

71

more texture, by showing each position her legs pass through instead of just throwing them high. It is more interesting. Fedorova hasn't been corrected much, and Hall is judged only by how much she has learned from the other's mistakes.

Balanchine continues to choreograph by demonstrating steps on the closest dancer. When he was younger, Balanchine danced every step when choreographing, but now he shows just as clearly and sensitively with gestures, finding security if he has someone who can easily translate these gestures. "When I can't move anymore," he once said, "that will be the end."

Balanchine begins to make a tableau of the four women as Victor Castelli and Christopher d'Amboise enter dripping with sweat from a rehearsal down the hall. Dunleavy explains their walk through the kicking limbs as Balanchine devises how the women will begin. He starts with Fedorova in the center and builds from there. When the pose is set he fiddles with the detail, standing back two or three times. Working up close, he can tell how this little picture, as a whole, will look from a distance. Adjusting Freedman's legs, Kumery's arm, Hall's body angle, Fedorova's head, he gradually builds the architecture he wants. Not one woman was in a pose such as would be found in the tableaus of romantic ballets. This was classical design with obtuse symmetry.

Gazing only long enough to memorize the tableau, he breaks the group apart by having Hall leave. She runs downstage diagonally toward the mirror and takes a separate pose reacting to a new pose of the central figures. After a brief adjustment, Balanchine smiles at her understanding. Hall glows proudly.

"When she goes, you do change," Balanchine says to the central three, before leading Kumery diagonally downstage opposite Hall and has her take a lunging pose that stretches her body. After much work changing the positions of the two remaining dancers haven't piqued his interest yet, so he asks for music and all of them return to their original positions.

"All together, please."

Boelzner plays the few dissonant chords in the formal *menuet*. Balanchine snaps his fingers when the girls are to break. Hall rushes back to her right, as though she were a limb broken from the statue. Kumery is led forward and forms another extension of the design with the two women switching into different positions on center. Simultaneously, Hall *bourrées* up the side of the room. The choreographer mutters something to himself. He has Kumery and Hall switch places. "Better. It was not interesting before."

Balanchine spends quite a few minutes coaching Freedman to rise smoothly from her pose to a *bourrée* in as short a time as it takes the first two women simply to switch their weight from their positions and move forward.

While he has them all continue into swirling patterns, the choreographer eventually develops a large square by walking to each dancer and painstakingly plotting her course. They cannot comprehend his design until it is completely assembled, a mystery dancers are accustomed to.

The silver-haired associate conductor, Hugo Fiorato, arrives and listens attentively to Boelzner's playing. Fiorato began his association with the company as concertmaster under its first conductor, Leon Barzin, during the time of Ballet Society, the forerunner of the New York City Ballet. His manner is gentle and congenial.

"From the beginning, maybe," Balanchine says, nodding in acknowledgment to the conductor, who has served loyally for over thirty five years.

With Balanchine's suggestion, Dunleavy shows Victor Castelli where to stand as Christopher d'Amboise, the understudy, watches closely from the side.

After asking a few questions pertaining to whether or not some steps are on pointe, and receiving a definite yes from Balanchine, everyone takes his place and starts from the beginning. The run-through has many stops again, having to do with the execution of technique rather than correcting timing or style. Castelli has plenty of time to learn the necessary progression of his walking steps. Although he can fly across any stage, like many dancers he feels uncomfortable walking —rather like a racing car caught in city traffic. The rehearsal stops when the steps end. So does the music.

"Gut," says the choreographer to the conductor.

"Ja gut." Fiorato, who gave his first recital in Frankfurt, beams back.

"Ja wohl," replies Balanchine, before turning to his ballerinas.

In the few minutes left he experiments with having them cross from one corner to the other. But decides instead to have them move backward toward each other to keep their square foundation. They check the mirror to avoid bumping into one another. By the time they get to the stage they will have the necessary perspective on the space.

As the dancers leave this session, they are faced with a warning that Rosemary Dunleavy has placed on the new rehearsal schedule: BE ON TIME TO ALL REHEARSALS, ESPECIALLY TCHAIKOVSKY REHEARSALS. Ter-Arutunian is seen racing down the corridor in search of Balanchine.

GIGUE

Victor Castelli stands alone, waiting. Hardly moving at all, conserving energy, his mind is pacing.

Light does not reach the chasms in his face. He is intense, with narrow eyes. Black, formfitting practice clothes sheath his slender ribbons of muscle. His eyes flick to the opening door.

Boelzner walks past the dancer and gives him a sideways glance. His teasing hello draws only a thin smile from the soloist. Hubert Saal, music and dance critic of *Newsweek* magazine at this time, remains in the same chair where he has observed company class. During the class Balanchine had made a point of telling his stories extremely clearly, in the journalist's direction, to spoof misrepresentation by the press. It was all good-natured, however, for the two had been friends for some time. When it was fashionable to say that Balanchine had lost his muse and originality, Saal had been a loyal defender, all during those years following Suzanne Farrell's departure and before the now-legendary Stravinsky Festival in 1972.

Castelli kicks his own head from behind, managing to release tension.

"Can I hear the music before he comes?" Castelli asks Boelzner with measured calm.

It was an allegro in 6/8 time, with many contrapuntal accents. What took Tchaikovsky four days to write was over in little more than a minute. Castelli remarks on the speed of the tempo.

Balanchine comes in and immediately asks the dancer to go to the center of the floor then stands before him with his arm raised. He extends the other, bends his knee, crooks his elbow, and juts out his hip. It's an exaggerated position in the *commedia dell'arte* style; the same style Balanchine used in his ballet *Harlequinade*. The costumes the little girls modeled last week came from the same ballet.

Balanchine experiments with the dancer's wrists and hands until he has them curling and rotating exactly the way he wants, before going on to stamp out a combination of steps, with bent legs turned in, then out. First he asks for both hands up as in an Irish jig. But keeping the steps the same, he then asks Castelli to fold them across his chest in the Russian folk style.

"Maybe come forward, then go back," Balanchine suggests. Castelli again tries the tricky combination. With this change, and the addition of the piano, one senses an underlying and subtle rise and fall in the music as the dancer moves upstage and downstage. It's a good example of how Balanchine prompts the viewer to hear what has not been heard before.

Castelli masters the next combination of intricate, quick-changing steps, but there is a silent beat that connects the two combinations. It is always difficult to stop the impetus of movement, keep the count of a silent beat and start on time as quickly as one has stopped—without looking as though one has hiccupped. However, the dancer runs into trouble only when he tries to connect a *pas de bourrée* to a step that Balanchine taps out to a syncopated "chugging" step—weight on his back foot and alternating between heel and toe with his front foot. This simple-looking Russian folk step along a diagonal doesn't come naturally to Castelli.

In Dunleavy's absence, Balanchine resorts to explaining it the best way he can by showing it himself. Again the dancer doesn't grasp it. Balanchine dances with more and more passion, time and time again, until finally stamping loudly and with a flourish he goes all the way to Saal in the corner. He finishes with the swagger of a Moiseyev dancer, enjoying himself thoroughly and bemused by the fact that Castelli can't catch the syncopation.

Beginning to sweat, Balanchine watches the dancer struggle. The last foray of the wiry Georgian has its effect. Probably what helped were the distinctive sounds of each of the three possible kinds of stepping. As in tap-dancing, listening for the rhythm and accentuation of sound is at times most advantageous when trying to decipher a combination. Another aid to any dancer would be familiarity with folk dancing and its traditions. Most Americans have no training in folk dance. With the exception of one year of English morris dancing, the School of American Ballet has not had teachers of folk dance since the great Russian character dancer, Yurek Lazowski taught his popular theatrical style. He once danced this *gigue*.

After accomplishing some extremely complicated combinations of syncopated steps, Balanchine shows Castelli a simple grapevine step, slowly marking the crossing steps with the soft bounce of an Israeli folk dancer, keeping his shoulders square and twisting his hips. He then adds a syncopated stamp of the Balkan style. The classical dancer doesn't begin to understand until Balanchine says, "It is like a *pas de bourrée*."

"More energy. BAM!" Balanchine says, scrunching his body, squinting his eyes and stamping his foot, before smiling back to Saal. Castelli dances. After another intricate circle, they continue into a series of tricky backward jumps with the feet flexed, before Castelli finishes with a long series of Russian-style heel and toe steps to the corner.

Balanchine asks for the whole section from the beginning. Castelli doesn't repeat any old mistakes though he does make a few new ones. But after correcting those, he dances the *gigue* straight through, mastering the fastest footwork yet devised for the new ballet.

Castelli is red with exertion through his olive Mediterranean complexion. Balanchine walks to the pianist and checks the score of "Eine Kleine Gigue," composed by Mozart in Leipzig; its ninety-six beats to the minute give Balanchine concern. "There is a second section. Then the whole thing repeats. A lot for one person. . . . Maybe a rest step," he murmurs to himself. In previous versions of the ballet this dance had not been presented as a solo.

By the time Balanchine walks back to Castelli he has an idea. Dunleavy enters from her rehearsal of another Tchaikovsky Festival ballet. Balanchine is already forming a large semicircle arching on a slant toward a part of the stage his dancer will not have used. It is essential to fill the frame of space. In the first section, he placed a step to every beat of the 6/8 tempo. Here he is trying to place the foot down on every third beat. It should be less taxing. Blocking the pace along an imaginary time line, Balanchine strives for a solution.

Castelli and Dunleavy follow closely for insight. Balanchine steps and swivels once for two beats whereas Castelli steps and spins twice. Balanchine lets him continue to translate in this way as he sees how well the dancer alternates the turns up the side of the room. The "rest step" had not become one.

In keeping with the feet landing on every third beat, Balanchine has his pliant soloist jump high over one leg in the far corner, before returning past center in a series of high and moving jumps with the arms to the side at shoulder level as the body plunges forward. "Like a bird," Balanchine announces with an open-eyed stare, hunching his shoulders and stretching his arms as would an owl.

Soon, Castelli finishes with a leg-splitting *sissonne* into an elegant standing pose. But Balanchine isn't finished. Neither is the composer. The dancer turns to Dunleavy with a mock look of fright when Balanchine returns to the score for refueling. Already the dance is more than the usual length of a classical male variation. Dunleavy asks the dripping dancer to show her the steps she missed while the choreographer studies the music. Their loud patter is obviously contrapuntal to what Balanchine is reading, yet, in a few minutes, he returns full of ideas, dashing around in a circle and crossing his feet in front of himself with bent knees. "Like football," he says, coaching Castelli. The step looks most like a jig. It is now alternating to the music's every beat, as opposed to every three.

After another series of the "rest step" from the opposite side of the stage, Balanchine goes on to combine a sequence of quickly syncopated Russian folk steps before switching to large jumps. Castelli uses his great elevation to move horizontally through the air to land on exact spots, designated by the choreographer, which will carry him back upstage. Finally pleased, Balanchine has him rush down center in time to every beat and finish with another large split *sissonne*. This time it is to the knee. Castelli would not have cared if it was to his head. He was numb from the work.

In the run-through the most challenging aspect of the dance became clear. The music keeps the same tempo throughout, with various inflections of tone. Balanchine's combinations play off the tempos with many interesting rhythms that don't slow the pace. Castelli is to start on half beats or let one or two go by after building up much speed and momentum before starting again at a different beat or direction. It is similar to the challenge Andersen faced in his first variation, the abrupt changes of timing, strength, control and action. By the end of the rehearsal, Castelli is kneeling with his hands on his hips as if to keep his heaving chest from collapsing.

Balanchine is beaming. The dance is over. He starts to the piano, but Dunleavy stops him to ask a question. "Mr. Balanchine, remember yesterday you had the boy walk through the girls in the *menuet*? He started way in the back. Now he is up front."

"Yesterday means nothing. I didn't know where the variation would finish. Only that girls come in on the last bars . . . ta ta de dum."

Balanchine walks to the center of the room, where Castelli had stood. The dancer looks back, his dance bag weighing down one shoulder. Balanchine stands tall with his eyes the level of the first balcony, and says, "He will finish here . . . and the Mafia will applaud him." They laugh. "Maybe even shoot him—especially if he's lousy."

After everyone leaves, Balanchine turns to Dunleavy, still full of whimsy, and says, "You know, I had a dream last night that everybody forgot the steps."

MENUET

Fedorova, Hall, Kumery and Freedman are guarding against Balanchine's nightmare. Their rehearsal in the Practice Room later that afternoon has not yet started so they mark their steps learned yesterday, with Dunleavy assisting. The dancers talk and argue directions as they dance easily, without the pressure of dancing full force in Balanchine's presence. They remind the woman opposite of mistakes or forgotten steps or double-check the person in front, or check themselves in the mirror. At times, Dunleavy points to one dancer out of synchronization in the formation, or out of time from the others. When Balanchine arrives, all discrepancies are sifted through but one.

"Which is it, Mr. Balanchine? This?" says Dunleavy, squeaking through a combination starting with a *piqué arabesque* from a *révérence* position. "Or this?" dancing the same but with a slight pause and added *coupé*.

Balanchine stares at her vacantly, not ready for her matter-of-factness. "Which version do you like?" he asks.

"The first," states Freedman.

"The second," says Kumery.

"Let me see together with the music," he suggests.

Balanchine places himself equidistant from the two women and has them dance to the music simultaneously. When they finish, Freedman asks, "On which note is it that we start?"

"The second way is right," says Balanchine, ignoring the question.

Unperturbed, Freedman asks, "Can we go over what we did yesterday with the music?" Balanchine nods and leans against the front barre.

The music helps refresh their memories of the sequential combinations more readily than the continuity of the steps. Within Balanchine's choreography the steps usually flow as naturally as walking from one foot to another; essentially that is how he worked. The challenge for the dancer is remembering the sequence of combinations. It is especially hard in a piece like this *menuet* in which Balanchine worked only four bars at a stretch, making as many bridges between the combinations.

Boelzner stops where yesterday's rehearsal left off, and Balanchine steps forward to Freedman after spreading out yesterday's square. She waves to Patricia Neary, a former company ballerina who is visiting from Switzerland, where she is Artistic Director of the Grand Theatre Ballet de Zurich. Freedman started her career in Neary's company.

"*Développé* to the side," Balanchine says, gesturing to Freedman's right leg. She is noted for the step. It is easy to see why, as she easily lifts her leg along her standing leg and extends it until her toe is well over six feet in the air. Her short torso makes her leg seem even higher as she holds her position a foot above her head. Saal, still in the theater after the end of Castelli's rehearsal, is clearly impressed.

Taking her accomplishment for granted, Balanchine makes his way around the square to Fedorova. But her wonderful extension is hidden. He cures that problem. "Make *écarté*, please," he announces. All the dancers turn slightly. Their legs do not parallel the perimeter of the square but angle toward the center, which will let the audience see the line of each leg separately.

Balanchine has Fedorova bring down her high leg and point it behind herself. Then he asks for a quick switch in the lunging position onto the first leg. She now faces straight forward. Knowing as he does every attribute of his dancers, Balanchine asks her for one of her most beautiful steps. "*Penché*," he says quietly.

The willowy dancer, once a princess in the Pennsylvania Ballet's version of *The Nutcracker*, now raises her straight back leg up and arches her torso forward with simple grace. The three others sigh and follow before Balanchine quickly shows a variation of the switching lunge. It looks like yesterday's *révérence*.

Staying with Fedorova, Balanchine asks for an *attitude* turn. She rises on pointe with her lifted back leg curved at the knee. The others quickly practice a few before Balanchine walks up to each of them and patiently waits for perfect mastery of the step. He changes arms from one girl to the next as different pictures of the step come to him. They all have to watch for the latest version.

"Okay. *Chassé* through each other and do *attitude* turn," Balanchine says, leading Fedorova and Freedman abreast of one another to pass the other two dancers coming from the other direction. One pair of women is asked to dance a count later than what was shown, unlike yesterday, when two counts separated pairs of dancers. This same kaleidoscopic effect was achieved but now it is more finely tuned.

Balanchine is working right along with the music at an unstoppable pace. During the very brief pauses the dancers' faces show concentration as they try to remember every step. There have been no short reviews as yet. Using four bars of music at a clip, the choreographer shows each combination separately to each woman, experimenting and using each one's individuality for all.

After many designs of passing through, around, under and over one another, this extended *menuet* takes a more formal tone. Balanchine has them stand in line briefly and curtsy to one another, framed by their rounded arms. When that is understood, the line is broken simply into a new formation and they finish with a deep *révérence* to one another.

Forming another line, Balanchine breaks into a pattern from half an hour ago, and catches the high-reaching, almost impercepitble rotation through the body and hips that Fedorova accomplishes when making his movement into her own. A ripple rolls slowly through her back to her neck. He lets her continue again before he cries out.

"That's it! Good. See now, Nina will show."

The quiet young woman shrinks from the others, managing somehow to look awkward and gangly.

"Music, please."

Fedorova dances the sequence. Everyone applauds. She blushes.

"That's Nina's step. I'll mark it right here," Balanchine exclaims, and marks it with a flourish on the score. Moving quickly to the next phrase, Balanchine asks them to curl around themselves intricately before forming another line. When they have achieved this they look at each other as if they had arrived by magic carpet. With no time to think further the dancers are asked to turn their legs in rather than take the classical outwardly rotated position. When the music starts, they run on pointe to their new pattern.

"No. Let me *see*, please," Balanchine says. "Feet are dead. I want feet alive." Instantly the women run toward him on pointe. Saal sighs. "Faster," Balanchine urges slapping his thighs with both hands in a blur of speed.

Having practically rushed into his lap, the dancers start again and drum toward him in unison with their feet scooting ahead of their bodies as horses might in dressage. Balanchine hunches forward, focusing on the speed and gesturing for more definition in the feet. He has said that pointes for women should be like elephant's trunks: strong, flexible and soft—also very pretty.

"That's right," he explains, slapping his sides and smiling beguilingly at his visitors. The dancers return to their places. Boelzner plays the new phrase and the four run with life, circle, then make a straight line. The ballet master has them turn out their legs once again and dance to one another. Now they turn into ladies of the court: they are no longer a line of bouncing chorus girls. Balanchine isn't afraid of incorporating any appropriate dance form.

To a strong chord in the music, a request is made for an explosive jump in opposing directions to a *révérence* in the opposite direction. Most often the leg-splitting and arm-extending *sissonne* separates a group that is in such close proximity—the "tutu distance" of two feet. But Balanchine wants the unusual; the dancers will jump toward each other.

"Cross please," he asks the two women in the center of the line, but one of them kicks the other. Apologies are made and they try once more. After a number of tries and a bump of bottoms, Fedorova and Freedman begin to bristle.

"Mr. Balanchine," Dunleavy calls, "maybe if we use the other leg there won't be any problem crossing."

"Yes, but then it will be like anything else," he replies, "the *croisé* leg is much better, more interesting."

His point is clear. The crossed position of the limbs along with the crossing of the inside two figures gives much more depth to the picture than a safer and flatter position. Freedman will have to angle the direction of her jump so that her rear legs will not kick toward the back corner of the room, but toward the side wall, so Fedorova can pass behind in midair.

A necessity in the corps de ballet is each dancer's adjustment to the other's space. It is a hard discipline. Often a corps member must sacrifice the movement he or she might like to dance to maintain the correct choreographic alignment. It is always a challenge and fun to fly or spin across the stage and pass through the correct hole of an oncoming line of dancers; but to be forced to cut down energy during performance for the sake of keeping place in formation can make a dancer feel as though he or she is not performing up to capacity, or will never be seen at his greatest advantage. On occasion stubbornness or forgetfulness has led to calamities such as midair crashes.

The following combination gives Freedman pause; her own body structure—her extra long legs and short torso, under normal circumstances attractive and advantageous—now cause trouble. Balanced on the tip of toe shoes that were designed to glide rather than grip, the disproportionate length and weight of her legs dominate and it is hard for her small frame to control the swinging action of the new step. Balanchine has her repeat it time and again until she controls the force of her leg to counter the delicate shift of weight. Her positions eventually become more exact. Balanchine steps back and watches the four women. They are each very different. Although all four women are tall, Balanchine already knows their individual characteristics and keeps those in mind when developing his initial ideas. He knows who jumps like a gazelle or lands like a cat; which ones are as strong as bulls and which dash like cheetahs; which bodies are chameleon and which unchangeable. This time Kumery was like a Persian cat; Hall, a quarter horse; Freedman, a foal, and Fedorova, a deer.

All the dancers stare, eyes wide, when Balanchine asks for a run–through—from the top. There has been no review of steps in two hours. However, by the time Boelzner has finished playing, and they have laced the dance together, not a single mistake is made. Dunleavy beams with pride.

VARIATION X

—————————— ह्ल्र ——————————

"The mirror is another person. Don't rely on it," says Balanchine in class the following day. It was good advice for dancers who had the bad habit of correcting themselves from what they saw instead of relying on their own sensitivity and feeling. In the past when Balanchine felt that his richly metaphoric stories were not understood by a new member, he would ask long-time principal dancer Jacques d'Amboise to "explain in plain English." However, today during the jumps he explains to an apprentice the exact way to land which makes it possible to move more quickly and fluently to the next position or jump.

"Knees should be over toes, weight over front of feet." The woman looks uncomfortable with her heels up. Balanchine lowers them slightly off the floor just enough to slide in a piece of paper. The heels appear to be on the floor, but a prehensile action produced through the feet gives enormous strength and leverage enabling a dancer to fly in any direction. Balanchine has been criticized for this by those who advocate placing the heel down on the floor for maximum stretch of the Achilles tendon.

Dancing on his heels in *demi-plié*, Balanchine clowns, looking like a bowlegged cowboy in his blue satin Western shirt. "Everyone says I invented heels off the floor. But it was the way I was taught!" he says. One remarkable story of his days as a student in the St. Petersburg Imperial School was that just before classes, he and his fellow students were made to wear chalk under the heels of their ballet shoes; if the chalk was missing at the end of class they would be whacked with the teacher's stick.

In "the office" downstairs Balanchine, manager Edward Bigelow, and four men in suits ask a dancer to try on a pair of shoes newly designed by Balanchine. The four men from Capezio's pass the dancer's own shoes, made by the competitive Freeds, between them as four horn players might a kazoo. They ask the dancer about the feel of different parts of the shoe. She can't judge fairly, for the shoe is the wrong size. Concerned, the cobblers begin to stop other dancers for opinions. But Balanchine insists that they make a new pair, in Farrell's size, for her to determine the soundness of the new design.

This little scene will affect thousands of dancers, just as did a trial test last week of a new floor, which turned out to be for the Kennedy Center. Balanchine said the company would not perform there again until they had a suitable one. Even when the shoes are complete, professional dancers will always have their personal shoes custom-made within the new line of the shoe's basic design. However, undoubtedly, with Balanchine's rare knowledge of how a woman's foot best works inside the construction of a toe shoe, the ones he chooses will be most comfortable and flattering.

The far-reaching nature of this episode is similar to former dancer Patricia Neary's visit yesterday. She had come to see the ballet school's performance to find a few dancers for her company. She also wanted to speak with Balanchine about getting some of his ballets for her company's repertoire, already filled with as many Balanchine ballets as it is stocked with former company dancers and School of American Ballet students. Almost every ballet company in the world has Balanchine's ballets, given free—though only to whom he chooses and when he chooses. And when they are given, usually a member or ballet master of the company goes to "stage" it. Like Lincoln Kirstein, Balanchine feels they belong to the world, to all those who an appreciate them. Their web of disciples and those disciples' companies and schools is an empire that has more influence over the ballet world than the largest conglomerate has over the business world.

The sweltering bodies have now cooled. Down the hall from the businessmen, where Leland was teaching a ballet with the aid of a videotape, Dunleavy and Castelli are teaching Christopher d'Amboise the *gigue* from *Mozartiana* as has been done for centuries, by copying gestures. The understudy gets the steps quickly but still needs to memorize the continuity. D'Amboise is feeling more secure with the feet; it is time to stress the exact positions of the head, hands and fingers. Castelli is very helpful with the details. On the first step d'Amboise achieves the correct curl and delicacy. But the simple weight of d'Amboise's heavier bones, as opposed to Castelli's finer ones, gives each gesture a more robust look, which seems inappropriate.

One of the riddles of dance is that a role developed on the body of one dancer forms a very different picture on another's. Balanchine's original model is the ideal and subsequent dancers have to find their own strengths within that image. Copying will never be as successful to any audience who has seen the original. Many times Balanchine solves the problem by changing his original work for the new dancer. Occasionally this has irritated the originals upon their return. For whatever Balanchine did last was considered, by the dancers, the inevitable evolution of his vision. However, Balanchine did not share that view. He made major changes in ballets already recognized as masterpieces.

Young d'Amboise quickly learns in forty minutes the ninety-second dance that took Balanchine one hundred five minutes to create. The first section goes quite well, with the young dancer dancing the Russian step with as much confidence and bravado as Castelli. But with the small interchanging steps, his feet, though on time and precisely placed, do not have the sting of Castelli's finer shaped arches.

He gets a third of the way into the run-through when Dunleavy directs him to dance the "football step" over again. Already these cross-switching *emboîtés* have a slang name. It is a shorthand code, commonly practiced in the company, between dancer, choreographer and rehearsal pianist. Instead of singing the needed phrase, a picturesque cue is written on the score. Balanchine thought of the two in the *gigue*, the "bird," where Castelli jumps forward on angle with his arms spread, and this "football" step, where the dancer moves laterally in a circle with crossing flicks of the feet as though trying to kick a round football. Balanchine makes a game of naming steps. One of his more famous cues is the "chicken step," danced by the two female leads and the corps of eight in *Concerto Barocco*, to Bach's double violin concerto. In Jerome Robbins' *Goldberg Variations*, the same step is performed by the four principal male dancers of the first section. Robbins calls it the "Barocco" step. But male dancers stick to "chicken," as amused by dancing this famous women's step as was Robbins when he decided to have four men dance it. The more inappropriate the name to the setting, the more fun it is.

D'Amboise, in his usual self-demanding manner perseveres by asking Dunleavy and Castelli to keep silent and allow him to get it on his own. He struggles through four more times with Boelzner moving up the tempo every time. He finishes a half-hour earlier than the scheduled ninety minutes. While resting at long last, d'Amboise asks, "Where does this dance fit in the ballet?"

"It comes before the *menuet*, and then Suzanne and Ib have eight variations and a *pas de deux* before the finale," Dunleavy answers. It was the first time both dancers had a clear idea of how it worked with the whole ballet.

"And Suzanne will be dancing with four little girls in the Ave Verum," Boelzner adds.

"Will there be singing?"

"No," someone jokes. "Suzanne will sing."

After working to keep one of his older ballets free of dust, Balanchine enters the Main Hall to continue on *Mozartiana*. The studio is alive. Everyone is anticipating portions of the ballet they have not yet seen.

David Richardson stands next to a line of five girls from the ballet school. They are about 12 years old. Among them is Dara Adler, the little Clara from the *Nutcracker* production of two years ago. Shiny-haired, they sit like a row of sparrows, sun-dried from their puddle bath. They can't stop staring at everything even though they are veterans of numerous children's roles.

Patricia Neary is sitting in her chair looking very official, except for the long curve of her calf muscle. It marks her as an insider, one who has danced. Hubert Saal is next to her. *The New York Times* reporter John Corry remains silently by the freight elevator across the room from them, his elbows resting on a crate. Boelzner waits at his post.

With great ceremony Balanchine unfolds a chair. He places one stiff hand before his face, dividing his eyes. He is playing surveyor. He looks straight above, down at his feet, right side, left side, sets the chair exactly center before sitting down. He crosses one leg, leans back. He holds his head regally, his nose up as though ready to detect anything foul. He is aquiline, aristocratic. The studio grows quiet.

"All right," he says softly. "Maybe let's see what we have."

Dunleavy double-checks with him, then announces, "Okay. First it will be Victor, then the four women, and then Suzanne and Ib." Balanchine raises his hand. He is about to see his work for the first time. Everyone else waits for Castelli as he stands in place, alert for his cue.

These situations are often more nerve-racking than performances before an audience. Here the dancer is scrutinized by one's peers. Balanchine believed "Art comes from artificial; what happens onstage is fake, in the studio is what is real."

Bravely, Castelli takes his place, starts and soon begins to have trouble with the tricky timing of some intricate steps. Balanchine sits with his head now cocked, listening for the music as he concentrates on the feet of the dancer. By merely watching a dancer's feet on the floor he can tell if the balance is too far forward, back, to one side, or if the dancer is keeping time to the music. Balanchine snaps his fingers loudly, giving the tempo to be maintained or adjusted by Boelzner and rediscovered by Castelli. At the end, Castelli avoids Balanchine's now raised eyes and waits on his knee as the four *menuet* dancers walk to their starting places.

"And," says Balanchine, giving the musical cue. "Come in when he finishes," he calls to the women.

"You'll have to start sooner," seconds Dunleavy, as they enter a half beat too late. "It's a fourteen from when he starts coming forward," she advises. The next time they arrive at the exact moment that Castelli lands on his knee.

The *menuet* starts, with Castelli letting out a hiss of self-disgust after his exit. Apparently Balanchine was only interested in the continuity of the work, for the dancers' performance could have used more work. The young women provide a flow of their own. Balanchine directs only their spacing. The difference between the shallow thirty-five-foot-wide practice room and the deep fifty-foot-wide Main Rehearsal Hall requires many subtle adjustments by the dancers, who naturally space themselves farther apart than before. Balanchine now has them covering much more ground; main-

George Balanchine

10A&B
Working on the *pas de deux* with Ib Andersen and Suzanne Farrell.

10C
Balanchine taps out tempo as Ib Andersen and Suzanne Farrell dance.

Suzanne Farrell and Ib Andersen rehearsing *pas de deux* on stage.

12A   The ballerina and the balletmaster.

13A
Suzanne Farrell
in a *grand jeté.*

13B
Ib Andersen
jumps in
sauté en passe.

13C
Ballet Mistress Rosemary
Dunleavy, pianist and assis-
tant conductor Gordon
Boelzner and a dancer, on
stage.

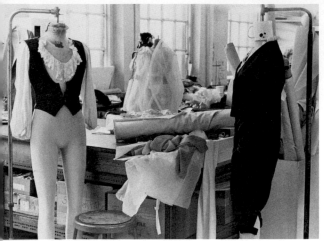

14A   Karinksa's shop, where all of the costumes for the New York City Ballet are made.

14C   Balanchine, designer Roubon Ter-Arutunian, production stage manager Ronald Bates and Lincoln Kirstein, co-founder with Balanchine of the New York City Ballet.

14B   New York City Ballet Musical director and conductor, Robert Irving.

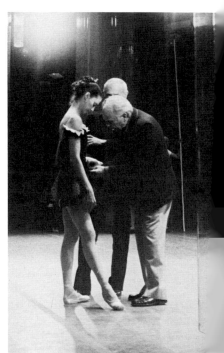

14D   Balanchine and Roubon Te Arutunian adjust the bodic on Suzanne Farrell's costum

15A Rosemary Dunleavy shows a step in the *gigue* to Christopher d'Amboise who took over the role of Victor Castelli after Castelli was injured in rehearsal.

5B Christopher d'Amboise dancing the *gigue*.

16   Balanchine talking with David Richardson, former dancer and supervisor of the children in *Mozartiana*.

taining the demure style of the *menuet* is much more difficult to achieve. Reaching the last step Balanchine choreographed for them, they pause momentarily for new steps.

"Next," he calls with a voice of a bored Broadway producer. At the wave of his hand the quartet disperses. Balanchine prepares himself in his chair for Andersen and Farrell. The two dancers roll their eyes at one another. It has been a week since they had last rehearsed the theme and variations and three days since they had danced their *pas de deux*.

Andersen doesn't need any subtle tugs of direction from Farrell by the time they come to the end of the brief theme. Already, looks of delight, interest and satisfaction cross the faces of everyone in the room. Balanchine sniffs his approval, cues Boelzner and snaps out his desired rhythm for Farrell's first variation. The ballerina does not miss a beat, finishing before the rivet of Neary's critical eye.

"Go on," Balanchine says.

To looks of surprise, Andersen bursts down the center and brushes through his awkward-feeling *balançois* step. He too masters his dance. By the end of Farrell's third variation and after Andersen's brilliant turns in the fourth—which brought whistles of amazement—the other dancers recognize the achievement during the past week of Balanchine and these two colleagues.

Farrell's opening step in the fifth variation has the female dancers in awe of her effortless and unique on-pointe, off-pointe *pirouettes*. Sixth variation, seventh variation, eighth— Andersen and Farrell finally stop, having danced pretty much as if they had worked on their solos every day.

Boelzner plays the music that calls to mind Balanchine's dancing like a girl from last week.

"Let me see," calls out Balanchine. He rises from his chair and explains the jumps of the running entrance to his four *menuet* women.

After charging down center and around Andersen and

Farrell, Balanchine slowly guides them through their patterns. After a few minutes they leap with the music, running and swirling in the design. Freedman and Fedorova bump and bounce off one another into a burst of giggles. Balanchine is impassive. He doesn't like his picture.

"Everybody come from back," he says, holding out his arms and gathering the women to the rear of the room. Taking two gently by the neck, he winds them into a new pattern as the other two follow from the opposite side. The design is worked with each pair dividing separately by one count, circling Andersen or Farrell, crossing the other and maintaining a balance of exchange and design. The opening step is all that has remained of the original thought.

They race through with the music. When they exit, Balanchine calls out, "*Chaîné* here!" and Andersen and Farrell jump to life and spin into their previously choreographed pattern. It's as though the four dancers were the wind and sent the two principals sailing around before settling into their *pas de deux*.

Boelzner continues into the ninth variation and Andersen supports Farrell as her leg slowly rises with a scale of notes. Balanchine moves to the edge of his chair, watching for the timing to the abrupt starts and stops in the next phrase of music. Though somewhat unsteady at places, Farrell applies the necessary attack and Andersen supplies just enough support. The breaks of time did not give Farrell any trouble. However, when her timing with Andersen's support was insecure, they hung on to each other and consequently provided a mixture of teetering excitement within the fractured delicacy of the *pas de deux*. Farrell tops off the mounting torque with the unsupported double *pirouette penché*, perfectly timed by Andersen's touch which swings her into the triple *pirouette posé*. The *pas de deux* finishes as she bumps out a hip.

Everyone breaks into laughter, all totally aware of the brilliance of the dance and dancing that has just taken place. Balanchine is the first to move, rising from his chair ready to continue. But instead of trying to piece together the ending of the unfinished *pas de deux*, he goes over to the row of little girls and lines them up.

These five girls had been chosen by Balanchine from a group of nine which Dunleavy selected from the cast of twenty who were dancing *A Midsummer Night's Dream* last night. The final choice has come. Richardson inches away from the girls.

"Stand tall," Balanchine says, slapping in his stomach with one hand and slamming his expanded chest with the other. The girls rise a bit taller, waver, endure Balanchine's focus.

Sharon Hershfield is separated from the others. She is the tallest. With her huge eyes she beseeches Balanchine, but he leaves her behind and leads the others to the center of the studio. Richardson places his arm gently around her shoulder and leads her to the back.

D'Amboise enters just in time for the start of new work. But before the door slams, the girls' mothers strain for a look into the room.

Balanchine asks for Castelli, and places him on center with two children on either side and methodically leads him and the little girls from their pose at center stage into sideways, rocking *balancés* that travel forward then back. The soloist and the children immediately catch the quick waltzing beat.

"Do four times," says the choreographer. They do. Richardson beams.

Immediately, Balanchine shows Castelli his combination by skipping down the center with his knees raised high, then has the children pivot away from Castelli, dancing the same skipping step. The inside girls get ahead of the outside girls and Richardson and Dunleavy rush in and lead them by the shoulders to explain the mechanics of a pivoting line.

"Then *sauté tour jeté*," says Balanchine, slapping his foot on the floor and twirling his finger in the air as he turns to face Castelli. The dancer nods with concentration and promptly joins the two steps before taking a preparation and hurtling his slender body into a leg-scissoring and half-turning leap.

They all repeat from the beginning, with the children tentative but dancing splendidly. Balanchine sits down and gestures to clear the space before him. The children look panicky, not knowing where to go.

"The same side that you stand next to Victor," Richardson tells them quietly.

Balanchine is waiting.

Castelli and the little girls enter and strike their pose, holding hands and balancing on the balls of their feet. No one wavers; no ankles wobble.

"Coda," announces Balanchine, and Boelzner starts the tenth and final variation on the theme. The dancers catch the allegro 3/8 tempo and fly forward.

"Now, giant girls!" exclaims the choreographer. The four female figures unfold from their resting positions. Balanchine stands in the rear of the studio requesting the music to be played and walks in at the desired time. The young women follow and pose as the children and Castelli did. It is the same picture developed in a grander scale.

With his "munchkins" lined up in front of the giants, Balanchine concocts quick-prancing and fast-beating steps. Although the children learn as quickly as the company members, they have difficulty with the speed. Relentlessly, they repeat until they have it mastered. Balanchine asks the name of the little girl after she has made a mistake.

"Dara," says the black-haired child with lovely eyelashes.

"Ahhh. Beautiful Russian name," Balanchine states. On her next try the striking young girl shows him the combination correctly.

Lisa Cantor was the next to make a mistake. She also elicited approval for having another Russian name. "Short for Elizabeth," says Balanchine, with such delight on his face that the children flub no more and respond with confidence.

With the new choreography just getting to the place in the music where Castelli has stopped, Balanchine walks away from the girls to where the dancer is still standing in place. Balanchine shows him a combination coming forward, then faces him with one hand on his hip. Drawing an assortment of pictures in the air he says, "Finish in pose, any way you like. You know something?" Castelli dances the spinning jump and assumes a pose similar to the opening of his *gigue*.

"What kind of turns would you like to do? *Grand pirouettes*, anything?" says Balanchine, luring the dancer to fulfill his wildest dreams. Castelli shrugs, not used to this freedom to invent. After mulling over hundreds of possibilities, he returns with plain multiple *pirouettes*. They are the best he has done in the ten years he has been with the company. There is applause. Castelli looks proudly to Balanchine.

"Maybe you should do tatata tee tee tee," the choreographer says impassively, after turning with one leg behind him in tiny hops before three-foot changing *emboîtés*. They are the same prancing hops the groups of girls danced in their combination coming forward. They offset one another perfectly when combined with the same music.

Balanchine then has Castelli leap upstage before having the tall women jump through the little girls and vice versa before circling around into another pattern that allows the children to finish front. When all this is danced to the music, it looks like waves of bodies lapping and overlapping each other; the man, the women, the children, all hopping in *emboîtés* and rocking in *balancés*. With only a few dancers, Balanchine has created a populous world full of a variety of characters. But another little girl is now confused.

"What is your name?"

"Tamara."

"Wow!" says Balanchine, delighted with all these little Russians; and especially with this one, who has the same name as his sister who was supposed to go to ballet school but whom he replaced, and also of the ballerina Tamara Toumanova, whom Balanchine discovered in a White Russian ballet school in Paris in 1931. Toumanova was then only a year or two older than this girl. Balanchine chose her as the ballerina for the first version of *Mozartiana* two years later. This coincidence brings the rehearsal to a halt. Balanchine asks everyone to pronounce the rolling *r* in Tamara. Only Farrell uses her tongue correctly.

Working methodically and patiently, Balanchine swings through the ensuing measures of music by giving each group of dancers different steps to match the interpolating nuances within the musical phrases. He sends his giant women tacking in zigzags down to the front and back again through the waves of little girls prancing underfoot.

With everyone finally posing, Balanchine brings on the prince and princess, somewhat hidden behind the high hedge of female figures. In the space on center, Castelli acknowledges their entrance with a bow of his head.

Andersen and Farrell are led forward, and Balanchine gestures the others to form a large semicircle with palms up in an introductory presentation. After a few tries, the couple and the shifting groups coordinate exactly. Farrell is asked to pirouette on center and finish in a pose with her partner's support. She spins within the security of his hands and stops exactly on the music with his squeeze of her waist.

"Bang!" stamps Balanchine.

The costume designer enters meekly. He is holding a sketchbook.

"Ah, Rouben Ter-Arutunian," says Balanchine, seeing him in the frame of the door. "Armenian. I bet nobody can say that name," he adds, as he ties himself into a knot pronouncing five extra "arus." Freedman promptly says it correctly, and flashes a grin.

The whole coda is requested. The Georgian and the Armenian sit side by side and watch the space fill with prances, waltzes, turns and crosses. The air is filled with celebration. The couple comes dancing forward, and they finish with a glorious flourish.

Amazingly, little time has passed.

Balanchine scans the frozen picture and sees a little blond girl with the wrong foot forward. He corrects her. She quickly switches.

"What is your name?" he asks expectantly.

"Amy."

PREGHIERA

After yesterday's "coda" rehearsal, Balanchine completes the unfinished *menuet* in ten minutes. In the remaining time, he sits and discusses sketches with the costume designer, making suggestions for costumes that had to be ready in three weeks. Ter-Arutunian wonders if plumes or hats should be worn by all the female dancers in *Mozartiana*, as they were in the original version designed by Christian Bérard; but Balanchine says no. After hearing a halfhearted request for combs, the choreographer ends the discussion with the statement "No, nothing. She will be angel."

Farrell enters the Main Rehearsal Hall still in full stage makeup from her matinee performance. Freshly powdered and costumed, she appears superhuman with no sign of having recently performed. Now Balanchine was going to make a dance for her. Balanchine had to do this ballet once more, because as Farrell said later, he hadn't yet gotten it quite right. She would dance Mozart's Ave Verum, Corpus [k. 618,] what Franz Liszt transcribed as his "À la Chapelle Sistine." On the piano Tchaikovsky's orchestrated version, called "Preghiera," in his fourth suite, rested next to the open music book of Mozart's original version. This is best suited for the rehearsal piano. The orchestral score is referred to by the choreographer whenever the instrumentation is necessary in order to clarify the texture of movement.

Boelzner is sight-reading the Ave Verum, tinkling a note every so often as his hands silently mark their course. Farrell sits on the floor tying her shoe ribbons as Balanchine enters quickly. His blue-and-white-checkered Western shirt is crisp.

"It doesn't matter . . ." he says, walking past and shaking his head toward her as if to imply she will not be needing new pointe shoes. "Nothing difficult will be done." She ties the last knots anyway, tucks in the ends under the wrapped ribbons and joins him at the piano. He conducts the tempo to the pianist.

"With Liszt we now have a Hungarian, an Austrian, and a Russian," says Balanchine, referring to the contributing composers. Sensing Farrell close behind him, he faces her and asks, "You're Catholic; how does it go?"

"It should be slow. It has all those Latin words in it—and they have to fit in."

"And what do they say?"

"It's about the Virgin Mary."

"Well," gasps Boelzner, beginning to rise from his bench, "that settles it then."

Chuckling, Balanchine returns to his position over the pianist's shoulder and reads the tempo marking aloud, "Andante non tanto. It should be andante, to go . . ." he says, walking away from the piano, "but not too fast, *non tanto.*" The pianist nods.

"Remember," whispers Balanchine, sidling up to the pianist as though he were a conspiring schoolmate, "tell Robert it should be slow. Because I don't think he goes to church."

After the jokes Balanchine asks for the same four young girls as yesterday. They rise from the corner where they have sat silently. The understudy has not returned. A little wiry blond girl loiters behind.

It has been decided to get another girl and have two understudies, one for each side, as is the policy of the corps de ballet. But one of them from a more advanced class at the school was annoyed by understudying the less advanced girls of the correct size; consequently, there is still one understudy.

Balanchine greets them warmly and repeats all their names, causing a row of smiles before asking the new girl her name.

"Francesca Filleuel." Its beauty lingers.

The high pressure of the previous few days of performances and rehearsals is always gone by Saturday or Sunday afternoon. Here now in the tranquility of the Main Hall at the top southwest corner of the theater, off to the side and one hundred feet above the stage, voices sound distant, music ephemeral. The pace downstairs and the clamor of the city outside seem foreign. Balanchine brings the little girls to Farrell, placing two on each side of her. She stands high on pointe with them on demi-pointe in ballet slippers, forming a semicircle. Balanchine stands before them whistling the first strains of music. It soon becomes evident that this Saturday is to be very special.

The girls have not been able to take their eyes off Farrell, calm and austere above them. The luster of her makeup emphasizes the sensitivity in her eyes. Yet its stage heaviness makes her seem a part of a magical world. Her gaze is leveled at Balanchine. He is communing with Tchaikovsky.

Slowly Balanchine straightens up from his distinctive slouch, and he starts to walk down center with an arm overhead. Farrell drifts after him, her body perfectly still as her feet flutter. Balanchine changes his mind and shuffles back to where he started. Then moving at the exact speed in which he expects her to follow, Balanchine crosses his forearms above his head and looks up. Slowly, slowly he walks in this position as though the light of a heavenly apparition is blinding him. She starts, a little too balletic, but when he touches his hand to one elbow to bend it more into a cross, she attains the exact effect. Months later, Farrell discovered where Balanchine found the position he gave her of the crossed hands. The madonna in the church she attended, the Blessed Sacrament on Broadway, held her hands exactly the same way. They had been there together many times.

Without a word he returns to two of the girls and pivots them from facing center to facing the wings offstage. Unused to working with the choreographer, the other two girls pivot in the same direction instead of the opposite. Farrell starts and they pivot into her path. Stopping, she bends over them and guides them in the right direction as a good fairy would two lost children.

They all repeat. Balanchine walks backward, facing Farrell, and slowly spreads his arms into a giving and open-palmed position. Farrell follows still looking heavenward, revealing, offering. With his elbows lifted and hands softly dropped, he gestures her backward by gently extending his arms. She wafts away.

A nod to Boelzner and he plays an enriched tone with an undercurrent of power. Leaning his head over a shoulder, Balanchine circles on the balls of his feet. Farrell repeats on pointe, her head and neck in the suppliant curve of a madonna.

In manner and tempo these simple walks are similar to a phrase in her shepherdess variation as Dulcinea opposite Balanchine's own *Don Quixote*. That role shed great light on her talent sixteen years ago. A hint of supreme spiritual love was present again today.

He takes four steps back to the side and bends one knee, while placing his other foot on the floor in front of him. One arm up, he indicates a backbend. Farrell steps softly and bends backward. Her torso uncurls until she arches in the air parallel to the floor, and stays level.

Helping her up, the choreographer tells a child to follow him. He steps as light as a young girl in her first pair of Sunday shoes. She chases after him and poses exactly as he does. He smiles.

Balanchine leads another girl next to the first. The other two are hesitant whether to proceed forward or not. They finally go when Balanchine crosses the studio toward them gesturing them to their places. He adjusts their heads and necks into the desired curve of the classical line.

Boelzner is cued. The music briefly grows from the last phrase heard. The children run silently and all are posed as Farrell's final furl unfolds. Balanchine reaches down and places his hand under her back, once more helping her up.

"*Arabesque*," he requests quietly. She switches her weight. Her back leg rises off the floor. Balanchine holds her wrists in the desired position and gives a little bend to his knees. She *pliés*.

Taking a few steps, Balanchine reaches into another *arabesque plié* in the opposite direction. She steps around with pointed feet and stretches into the same position as he watches with his back to the mirror. He shuffles backward to allow space, indicating to her to continue. She follows him with four languid *arabesques*, before she is asked to stand. The two figures form a huddle. The children dare not move.

Never turning from her, Balanchine begins to lead Farrell forward again and around the stage. She *bourrées*. They move as one—her toes flutter after his footsteps, both heads level. When their dance ends, he walks to one girl before he runs across the floor.

Tamara Molina traces his line but kneels clumsily as she switches to face the ballerina. Balanchine carefully shows her how to place her feet with one large step to counteract her forward momentum and enable her to swivel down with her weight on the other leg. After a few attempts she does it as if she were a cignet in *Swan Lake*.

Balanchine asks Farrell to come forward again, before he sends another sprite across her path.

Circling at the exact speed he anticipates her to travel, Balanchine leads her around the front of the stage before sending her toward the back of the studio, allowing the children to cross again. The spacing is timed perfectly. But with the addition of the new music the children have to rely upon Farrell's discreet flicks of the head.

With a loud boom, the doors open and Richardson and Dunleavy tiptoe to the side of the room to watch. Balanchine has his hands closed in prayer. As he lifts them high, he takes a heavy step, letting one foot drag. Taking another step, he swings his shoulders. His palms separate but his fingers form steeples. A third labored step. One more and he beckons Farrell. His voice is low and singing. She steps in time. He comes to her. He touches her gently, raising her arms slightly more ahead of her. Her body moves to his voice on the last two steps. The silence is absolute.

Standing in her path, Balanchine reaches over her head, murmuring directions and holding her arms in support as she slowly descends to one knee. He takes a step behind her, sliding his hold along her arms to her wrists. Her body yields as he drops her head back. He opens her arms. They continue spreading slowly, baring her breast and tender throat. An entreaty to God.

Dunleavy has her hands to her lips.

Balanchine places one set of girls to skim the floor and stand in a pose behind Farrell. Richardson helps guide the other two into exact position. Forming a semicircle, their arms are set by Balanchine with their hands overlapping each other's wrists. Flowers in a garland.

Balanchine moves off quietly calling for Farrell to repeat the slow step. He sings again for her. As she starts to kneel, he has the children form a curve behind her. A saint in a niche.

Balanchine raises his arms and Farrell rises. The children

are sent running with arms outspread "like birds" in circular patterns to the four corners.

Balanchine peels away and swings, whistling out his breath, to Farrell. She *bourrées* backward a few feet before he beckons her forward. He sends her back, then forward again. He asks her to repeat it all in one movement as though breathing in and out and in again. The music starts.

After Farrell assimilates the next combination, they waver side to side. The music begins and Farrell and the children pose in prayer. Farrell kneels. The children flutter around then softly join the prayer. The music envelops them. The ballerina's heart is open as she ascends and glides forward. Balanchine mirrors her movements. In time to Mozart, they pull together, expand and close. She shines under heavy lids of purple. Balanchine is intent. Farrell's brow creases, her mouth mourns. They separate, part, then close together. They stand, side by side, their hands clasped, the same spirit. Eventually Balanchine is able to turn once in place. Their intense communion remains as he walks to center and back upstage. After a twisting *soutenu*, Farrell *bourrées* closely after him, to where she began.

Leaving her side, Balanchine gathers the children, asking them to line up with Farrell. A nod to begin the music and this new phrase comes to life.

When repeated, everyone turns except one girl. Balanchine raises his voice. The little girl's eyes grow huge. His picture is no longer perfect. She misses again. He explains the counts and points out the exact one to turn on. Richardson gives her a discreet cue from behind and all turn together with the music.

With one foot remaining behind him on the floor, Balanchine begins an extremely slow lift of his arms and final curl of his hands. Tamara Molina's arms are too stiff; he asks for rounder elbows and prettier fingers. She soon gains the finish.

The music gathers its final surge. They have reached the

end of their movement, but the music lingers with three faint notes drifting away higher and higher and higher.

"Let's see how much time it takes."

The dance is run through twice more and Balanchine dances with Farrell each time.

"Last three bars wait. Then the curtain comes down so applause won't drown out music . . . very faint . . . very noble. These notes should be never-ending."

VARIATION X, CONTINUED

_____ ❧ _____

On Sunday, Balanchine starts a new ballet. *Mozartiana* is not finished, but all that remains is the finale; and the principal dancers for the "new Hungarian ballet," Adam Lüders and Karin von Aroldingen, are now available. It had seemed that, with von Aroldingen's character dance and ballet training in Berlin and Lüder's Bournonville training in Copenhagen, the two European dancers would easily understand the Hungarian music and folk qualities. But problems arise by Tuesday. As Balanchine choreographs, it looks more like work than enjoyment for him—a rare occurrence. There is no sparkle, no whimsy, only round shoulders and a furrowed brow from the drudgery of dancing for the lead and four backup couples over and over again. Sweating profusely, he drags himself down to his office at the end of rehearsal.

At the start of *Mozartiana*, an hour after the Hungarian rehearsal, Balanchine's face is still drawn. He looks at the clock; two more hours are scheduled. He straightens his hair. But as he enters the small space of the Practice Room all the dancers come to life.

Castelli stops his barre and stands in the middle of the semicircle behind Andersen and Farrell. He arrived stone cold from standing two hours at a mass costume fitting for another new Tchaikovsky ballet. Farrell rises onto pointe in her pose and Andersen supports her by the waist. He looks extremely pale.

"First *chaîné* down the center," Balanchine says to the ballerina, then stops her brilliant series of turns. In tandem they move around the room, alternating the feet irregularly, keeping time with the inner rhythm of the music.

Boelzner is cued and starts the cadenza with his right hand. Farrell circles as directed but the music wasn't finished, and she circles again. At the end of her whizzing turns, Andersen meets his partner and Balanchine breaks the line of dancers where the big and little girls stand beside each other. The semicircle is transformed into two straight lines with the company dancers on either side of Castelli. The two sets of little girls rush to Andersen and Farrell in the front row when they are told to hold hands in line, flanking the principals.

The transformation works perfectly after Farrell skirts the circle once more. Balanchine is already staring at the floor. He begins to take little steps to himself, and stops and starts many times. Looking up, he announces, "Everybody," but proceeds to show the combination only to Andersen and Farrell. The children watch from their difficult side angle and the dancers behind them fan out for a clearer view of the principals' feet. Balanchine is marking in place. It takes a few moments for the lead couple to understand the tricky combination. Finally and slowly, it is danced to the music by the three of them.

"Faster." Boelzner plays the combination up to tempo. There are too many steps to a measure. When the phrase was danced slowly it worked, but now a miscalculation by Balanchine is evident. He changes it to another baffling combination. A smile crosses his face as his dancers valiantly trip through the new sequence. "It is impossible," he boasts.

During the next ten minutes everyone tries to decipher the

combination. Their feet crisscross in a maze of steps, hopping with inventive irregularity as they move from side to side in counterpoint to the music. Balanchine demonstrates to Castelli and his four young women. The children attack the step courageously with Richardson learning it just in time to be of assistance to two of the little girls while Leland gives attention to the others. Dunleavy oversees Andersen and Farrell correcting each other. Balanchine rises from his chair every so often and shows the steps again. He makes another change just as it is about to be learned. Eventually the dancers learn the new version. But the children are still thrown. Boelzner marks "trouble step" in the score.

Though the children still have questions, Balanchine continues and asks Andersen and Farrell to turn in place. Then trusting that the children will learn the combination later, he proceeds to circle the young girls back while having the company women come forward and dance through their line, before they too pivot around and return upstage. Boelzner plays the part through before Balanchine asks that the two sequences be joined. Although previously warned, the children miss a silent first count, yet dance forward, a cavalcade of bobbing heads. The following sequence of turning principals and interchanging corps works better. But after the "trouble step" is repeated, the children shrug to one another. They plead to Richardson with their eyes and bow their heads before Balanchine. However, the choreographer is concerned only with the order and structure at this point. Each child wonders if Balanchine will remember her inability and consequently never take her into the company.

Susan Hendl, a soloist who has recently begun to "take" rehearsals, enters, and Dunleavy mentions to Balanchine that it is time to move to the Main Hall. Like a dutiful child, Balanchine rises from his chair and joins his dancers filing out the door. The hallway is mobbed by groups of dancers changing rehearsals, just as students change classrooms.

After the smaller studio, the Main Hall is like an open meadow. The dancers stride in. But Balanchine staggers over to Farrell, playfully, and places his head on her shoulder, his arms dangling like ropes. For a long time she pats his back. Finally he lifts his head. There is another hour to go.

Everyone reviews the coda until the last point of choreography. But the following sequence is as hellish as the one in the practice room. It is nicknamed the "*échappé* trouble step," with its hops of separated legs, interspersed with a myriad of crossing feet. The children manage this better than the other but it gives Castelli terrible trouble.

After all is settled, Balanchine has the corps back away with Farrell spinning in Andersen's hands. She is asked to finish with her back to the audience with Andersen facing and supporting her to one side. The surprise ending takes the breath away just as did the corresponding pause in the music. The silence and sudden immobility have tremendous power.

The corps is brought into a tighter rectangle, after Andersen is asked to lift Farrell to the back on center. Immediatelly, the choreography has Andersen partner her in consecutive twisting turns; they keep the eye of the viewer from the subtle shift of the group. As in many Balanchine ballets the ensemble is active during the principal's best displays; he rarely sets up a solo spectacle. In a sense, the ballets are democratic: like nature—trees do not stop blowing in the wind when a sparrow sings.

All the dancers are in position once more to rush downstage en masse, although Richardson is still answering questions and coaching two of the children about the first "trouble step."

This new combination does not look as difficult to learn as the previous one as Balanchine weaves down the floor. Behind him a clatter of toe shoes follow in a cacophony of independent taps from each dancer picking up the sequence at her own pace. Today, Balanchine is altering the choreography much more than he has since he started working on this version of *Mozartiana*. He extracts, develops, rearranges, many of his initial movements. He appears tired as his vitality is sapped by the changes he is making in his ballet.

The dancers show him their interpretations after he slowly settles into his chair. The steps are not as intricate as before but achieve the same effect.

"Lift your legs higher, please," Balanchine calls out to the corps dancers. "*Attitude* up here," he says, remaining in his chair and lifting a leg high above the knee of the other. "Don't just cross your feet. Otherwise it looks like everything else." The sequence instantly reveals its hidden character.

Balanchine follows the charge forward with a full retreat. Then stalls their momentum with another small combination before dispersing them to the sides. The children pose momentarily. Castelli and Andersen continue back with large leaps and dance sets of multiple *pirouettes*. The four women are corralled into a small semicircle and Balanchine finds a step for them that balances the new turns of Farrell's. They will alternate *passés* with her *pirouettes*.

After much study of the separate groups of dancers, Balanchine times each combination mathematically so that there is a relationship among them. This makes the different layers of the music clear to the eye. It is one of the most essential aspects of his work: a choreographer can't invent rhythms, he explains; he can only reflect them in the dance.

By the time Balanchine has corrected and coached his dancers, there is not enough time to choreograph the finale, only enough to run through "for the brains." He weakly cues Boelzner. Farrell twirls around Andersen, keeping a smaller circle than she might have if the sequence were set here in the Main Hall rather than in the smaller practice room. She finishes and Andersen joins her and they take the children's hands. Castelli and the *menuet* quartet line up behind them as the music fades into a reprieve. Then with great concentration, the group rushes forward. The children start incorrectly on the silent beat once again but do not get caught and complete the "trouble step" perfectly. They smile as they pivot back, but frown in concentration when they dance the *échappé* trouble step. Farrell overspins. Andersen leans her away with an encouraging call from Balanchine. The still pale dancer gathers his strength and lifts the ballerina as she goes onto her flashing *pirouettes* before the music builds for another surge. The dancers extend their legs high in *attitude* just as Balanchine had asked. The little girls dash to the side as the two men take their places in the middle of the semicircle of females, who pose and dance while the principals turn in corresponding tiers of developed movements. The music continues until Andersen takes Farrell forward. The long and arduous preparation has yielded abrupt results.

The dancers catch their breath glad that the finale is so short. It doesn't sound as though there will be much more music. But time has run out and Balanchine slowly pushes himself off the chair.

Although Andersen has another rehearsal, he leaves for home and rest. The little girls will have supper with their mothers before their roles as bugs in tonight's *A Midsummer Night's Dream*. Boelzner heads for the sanctity of the company's pianists' room. Balanchine and Farrell leave together with her supporting him around the waist. He drapes his arm over her shoulder and rests his head.

VARIATION X, CONTINUED

Balanchine won't be teaching classes anymore. One of the many gifted teachers of the school, Andrei Kramarevsky, will be giving company class while Balanchine and ballet master John Taras, the usual teacher, devote themselves to their new ballets. Robbins, who has taught for short periods of time, is also too busy, as is Dunleavy and many of the other respected dancers who teach. It seems Balanchine taught class the last two weeks just to start his dancers off in the right direction this season. His influence must have been greatly needed, for the company's dancing shows a great renewal of life. A wonderful change compared with the last few seasons when he was often too ill to work. Now he is nurturing his company for the Tchaikovsky Festival.

Balanchine always claims that classes are exasperating for him—constantly having to make the same corrections, and, quite often, to the same people for years and years. Most disheartening for any dancer is when he says in class, "I tell you a thousand times. You correct a thousand times. And the next day?—it is wrong again! This I cannot understand." After which he shrugs, slaps his thighs and walks away asking other dancers to explain why, as they stand mute with guilt.

114

Besides the fact that his assistant, Barbara Horgan, suggested he slow down, especially after his appearance the past two days, there is at this point so much else to do that Balanchine has to move on from the classroom. He talks with Ter-Arutunian about costumes for a production of *The Firebird* for the Chicago City Ballet. The female Scaramouche costumes from *Harlequinade* have been sent to Karinska's costume shop, because the *Mozartiana* costumes will be patterned after them. More costumes for the *Pathétique* have been dyed. In the Hungarian ballet, Dunleavy has had to demonstrate the steps for Balanchine, because the men's movements entail a lot of jumping. And Balanchine not only has to keep watch over his new ballets, but those of the other choreographers and the ballets in the current repertory. He tried making jokes about his back, his knees, his eyes and hand, but he was in a lot of pain. Backstage, the smell from a truckload of plastic tubes permeates the air.

The pressure of the festival was condensed in the Main Hall. Reporters Hubert Saal and John Corry are present again on the lookout for everything. Robert Irving sits by the piano, a large and crucial symbol of unity. Boelzner rereads the music. Richardson quickly rehearses the children. Dunleavy sits in a sideways split to keep herself in condition while watching Leland teach Fedorova what the dancer missed yesterday. The others talk among themselves reviewing their parts. Eventually the cast volunteers to go through the finale with music. The Tchaikovsky Festival is only two weeks away.

Balanchine enters with a metronome, places it carefully on the piano and sets to work. The triangular timekeeper seems to stand watch over the room as the dancers take yesterday's formation.

"One," Balanchine says to two small girls, and quickly moves to the places he wishes them to run. Richardson guides the other two in the opposite direction. "Two," the choreographer counts, and beckons Fedorova and Kumery to where he stands. They jump in *arabesque*, just as the children had, and stand next to him. The other two women copy them, going in the opposite direction.

Farrell smiles at Balanchine expectantly, but he walks to Castelli in the rear of the studio. "Three," he says, and leads the dancer to the left of center and all the way to the front near the piano. "Four," he calls to Andersen, gesturing him to go to his right and end on the opposite side of stage from Castelli. Spreading his arms, Balanchine walks up to Farrell, takes her hand and leads her straight down the center into a horizontal line with the two men at the corners. "Five."

Stepping back, he observes the new formation, then places the two males just inside each set of little girls. Balanchine tells the four women to *piqué pirouette* to the center. However, on second thought, he asks Fedorova and Kumery if they object to turning to the left as opposed to the more natural right. He obviously prefers them all to be facing front when turning to finish behind Farrell.

Signaling in the two men, Balanchine has them kneel in front of Farrell, with Andersen closer to his partner. Their arms are arranged in various positions, then their bodies, before having them frame either side of the ballerina. He wants their arms to cross in front of her and curve overhead. The little girls are asked to come in closer and kneel, and the tall women rise high onto pointe and form looping arches with their arms as the little girls did in the Preghiera behind Farrell. In the final flowery baroque tableau she is like a stamen framed by petals of rounded arms and hands.

Boelzner is cued after Balanchine reviews everyone's counts. But everybody now finds himself counting double time as they had yesterday. "The counts are slow," says the pianist, and counts out the new slow ten, and a fast four. When the dancers have learned the music they won't have to count at all. Richardson counts aloud for the children. Andersen and Castelli *chaîné* in on the fast four, extending the twirling picture of the slower-turning female quartet.

Balanchine sits down, thrilled with the spinning finish to his ballet. "Bam!" he exclaims at the sharp ending. He is smiling. The dancers break their pose. It is done. The whole group beams back at Balanchine. "But there won't be a bang with the double basses," Balanchine says as an afterthought. "They can't make it."

"I think I saw a cymbal written in somewhere," says the pianist.

"No, no," declares Irving, correcting everyone. "There are only two clarinets and two oboes, and they won't make much of a smash." His authority seals the end of the ballet.

They run through the finale a number of times before Balanchine announces, "Let's do the whole thing from the beginning! Just walk," he tells the dancers, "but we do timing." And, facing the musicians, "Then remember, mark with metronome, then make tape of music—so no one can say it was neeever like that"—a familiar phrase in the company when a former cast member criticized a more recent one.

"We will start with Preghiera," he announces. It was actually composed as the third movement by Tchaikovsky and it remained there in Balanchine's first three versions to the score. Putting the soulful prayer first, Balanchine changes the whole mood and tone of the dance. It is more spiritual, reflecting his "Ode to Tchaikovsky." He planned *Mozartiana* as the first ballet of the Tchaikovsky Festival. It would set the tone. But he also put the Preghiera first because it gives Farrell some rest between very demanding variations. In an earlier version, her role was done by two ballerinas. Balanchine, as usual, was thinking both poetically and practically.

"The curtain will go up as the music plays," says Balanchine, and his hands float upward. "There is a little music before we will start. The dancers will be on. . . . No, wait. The applause will be so loud, it will destroy. We will have to wait

117

with the music until the applause stops; it will be the first time they see the beautiful set. . . . Tchaikovsky will probably be there with his entourage: Borodin, Moussorgsky, Cui, Balakirev, Rimsky-Korsakov."

Balanchine picks out a spot in the score eight measures after the beginning, where the small girls are to come on stage. Boelzner marks it. The choreographer calls out, "Count eight before."

Farrell stands on center as the children enter at the appropriate time. The girls pose on either side. Balanchine realizes that Farrell also has to enter and tells the children to start at the beginning of the music. They walk gingerly. He signals the ballerina, "Where the voice sings." It is the original eight bars into the score.

Hugo Fiorato enters. Balanchine tells him for the first time that the prayer is first. Everyone starts once again and Balanchine sits immobile, almost expressionless, as though he is empty now that the ballet is finished. The mood is haunting. Suddenly Balanchine taps the balls of his feet in a flurry, indicating to the children that he wants them to *bourrée* in place. The tiny steps in place make the girls shimmer rather than just be pretty. Balanchine has found another way to enhance his ballet. Farrell and the little girls float through their dance until the three notes fade away, taking everyone's breath with them.

Castelli rotates his ankles, knuckles and toes to release stiffness and anxiety before taking his place. "Play like we said," Balanchine tells Boelzner; "you know, I want to hear everything." The pianist plays as clearly as possible, trying to duplicate individual instruments of the orchestra with his fingers. The *gigue* seems slower than when it was choreographed. Castelli isn't complaining. His first rapid combination is much easier in the present tempo. But later in the variation, the slower tempo makes his higher jumps much heavier. When he finishes, Castelli states, "The music is a lot slower than it was."

"A lot? Noooo," retorts Balanchine.

Castelli has not budged.

"I can tell," Balanchine says, and proceeds to dance the Russian step he had shown the dancer many times over. He points out the syncopated stamping and announces, "This is the tempo. What do you think?"

Fiorato suggests, "It would be a better tempo like this," and beats a time for Boelzner. Balanchine sparkles as he dances again. It is the first time this week he has shown any spirit.

The *menuet* moves rather well with the expansive extensions and crisscrosses of the four females filling the whole room. Balanchine stops them only once. "You are to be like dancers, pretty, with legs like this," he says waving his arms before him. "Not like baseball players," he says, bending forward and clomping in long strides. "You are ladies. Dainty, beautiful." The music resumes and they dance that way, finishing in their *révérence* to each other.

Balanchine perks up and conducts as Farrell and Andersen enter on the theme. His tempos are matched by the pianist and the two dancers—elegant as they walk without placing their heels down. Although they are rehearsing, they seem to be performing. The way one danced in class and rehearsal was the way one danced on stage. There were no miracles after the curtain rose.

The two stop once. It is the same place where they had trouble in their very first rehearsal, when trying to remember the exact way of passing their hands behind shoulders and waists. It remains a sore spot. Farrell figures out the problem by sensing the feeling of relative muscle coordination to movements before and after the missing link. By the end of the theme, the two dancers have set the pace and style of the rest of the ballet.

With sublime aplomb the ballerina develops her brilliant series of quick-changing, off-balance, counter-angled combinations. Andersen skims through his first variation as Farrell does her second. Andersen has a few short mental lapses in his second variation, but catches them in time and does not have to stop. After his third variation, Andersen remains on his knee and leans forward on his elbows.

"Wasn't that one slow?" he asks. It was the time to speak up, since both conductors were seeing the completed dance for the first time.

Balanchine looks at the musicians and they play the music through again. "No," Balanchine replies.

"Well, I don't know . . . does seem slower," the dancer mutters, getting up and walking to the side. Balanchine lets him go, confident it will work out. Although Andersen was prepared and warm, he didn't have the spring he had, due to his mysterious illness. The first two variations, with their faster jumps, had not demanded the power needed to accomplish the larger leaps of this last dance.

Farrell's final variation now flows beautifully into the duet, but the corps misses their run-on entrance. Distracted by their giggles, the musicians look up from their scores. Balanchine doesn't see any need to stop the moving picture, until Freedman speaks for the quartet and asks to try it over again. This was only the second time they had heard the continuity of the variations.

They are allowed to complete their swirling patterns around Andersen and Farrell, who spin around and into the start of their *pas de deux*. On their second combination, Balanchine claps, halting the music.

He always stops here—just as every dancer in every ballet has a difficult spot, a choreographer has his, and this is Balanchine's. It is the first step in the *pas de deux*, where Andersen lunges to his left while maintaining his support of Farrell after she has stopped abruptly in *arabesque*. The step, not difficult except for its speed and abrupt halt, is attempted time and again.

Balanchine shows the technique, wishing Andersen to support her with only one hand at the finish since the other wrist touched her waist. The dancer accomplishes this but he is not far enough from Farrell. Although Balanchine does it with ease, over and over Andersen tries in vain. Finally Balanchine walks up to Andersen and measures the length of their arms from the shoulder. Though two inches shorter in stature than the five-foot-ten Dane, Balanchine has longer arms.

"Like a monkey. That's me," he says, smiling. "Let's go on."

The dancers repeat this sequence. Balanchine smiles again —the step works perfectly.

Throughout the rest of the *pas de deux* Balanchine sings along in the musical vernacular of classical scat while miming the violin breaks. Fiorato and the dancers heed these cues of musical intonations. The finale brings its waves of dancers, making the ballet seem much fuller than its actual eleven dancers. Soon, they are at the end, where they had started an hour and a half ago.

The rehearsal disbands with the conductors keeping in mind the tempos of the day. The metronome had not been used. The next scheduled rehearsal starts immediately. Most dancers will be busy the rest of the afternoon, including Andersen, who straggles out the door.

Before his next rehearsals, Balanchine, surprisingly, goes to Marika Molnar's physical therapy office. His hand has been bothering him for a week and a half. The trip is a surprise. Historically, he disapproves of treatment such as massage or ultrasound.

At the end of the day, designer Kermit Love squeezes into Balanchine's office with the best remedy of all: a new pair of angel wings.

KARINSKA

Late Saturday morning Farrell has an appointment at Karinska's. She is to be fitted for her costume for *Mozartiana*. On this May morning the costume shop is bathed in silver light pouring through a wall of windows. The seamstresses bow over their work in silence. A row of cutting tables fills half the room, looking like barges laden with exotic riches.

This airy studio isn't as large as the space Karinska occupied for years on 57th Street above the showroom of Maximillian Furs, but it was most convenient to the theater two blocks away. Since 1963 the New York City Ballet has, with the help of Ford Foundation grants, been the sole beneficiary of Karinska's skills, with the exception of one *La Traviata* at the Metropolitan Opera for her old friend Cecil Beaton. However, the studio was larger than her old 44th Street studio and most certainly more comfortable than her first in 1938, with one cutting table in a small studio in the original School of American Ballet on Madison Avenue.

Karinska's is a shrine to the ballet. Its founder, born in Karkov in the Ukraine, learned how to embroider at the age of 12. Pictures of old designs and costumes hang like icons in her office. They also fill a few vacant spots along walls crammed with bolts of fabric and drawers filled with buttons, brocades, braids, ribbons, feathers, jewels, ruffles, laces, gold and silver thread.

Ben Benson, the designer and present costume shop manager, leaves the dye room to look at a series of sketches on his desk. There are racks of new costumes for the festival and old ones to be copied or refurbished afterward. A small woman sits at one table sewing jewels on mesh and fine netting. On a large cutting table lie patterns for the many seamed bodices. The only sewing machine disrupts the silence as another seamstress sews white brocade to a white satin bodice of one of the many costumes for John Taras' *Souvenir de Florence*. Ter-Arutunian is checking a black satin tunic, trimmed with black velvet, cut at the waist and flared at the hips in baroque fashion. It fits the dress form perfectly and a slip of paper labelled "Castelli" gets pinned to the shoulder.

At this point, Andersen's costume is simply an array of cut strips, spread out in order, and waiting for their backing before being sewn together. Farrell's is hanging on a rack in the rear dressing room.

A few minutes later the ballerina walks through the front door. Ter-Arutunian leads her to the costume. When she hooks it over her own leotard and tights, she mentions that it is a little long, but that the bell shape is interesting.

Farrell twists her hips back and forth to see what effect turns will have on the look of her skirt, just as a male dancer would raise his arms and breathe deeply to test the comfort and look of his form-fitting tunic when lifting a partner. The speckled top layer of black silk point d'esprit swishes across the stiffer lace-trimmed layers of white tulleing underneath. "You know, this is my first black costume," she says to Ter-Arutunian. From her initial leading role with the company, John Taras' *Arcade*, she has almost always been in white; white, or certainly shades of it, in early works of Jacques d'Amboise; and in almost every one of Balanchine's—*Don*

Quixote, the Diamond Section of *Jewels*, *Meditation*. Even in the "black and white" ballets, so traditional to the company, Farrell was often in a white leotard: in Stravinsky's *Monumentum*, *Movements*, and *Variations* and in Xenakis' *Metastaseis* & *Pithoprakta*. However, Karinska once did make her a silky black dress for a gala party.

"Balanchine isn't going to like the V–neck. He usually prefers a scoop," Farrell states. The designer merely squints at her skirt and centers the layers of ruffles to match the centerpoint of the bodice. The seamstress adjusts the pink elastic shoulder straps, asking Farrell if she is uncomfortable. She nods.

Before the triple-angled mirror, the ballerina stands tall in yellow open-toed pumps—comical under the sober costume.

With the distinctive blue backdrop of the company, and Farrell always in white, Balanchine achieved the same effect he wants here, highlighting her in a rare black costume before a rare white setting.

Two more seamstresses come to admire their work before Balanchine arrives in a rush and quickly tests the feel of the four underlayers of white, lace-trimmed tulle.

"It's not what I want! Rouben, didn't I tell you the other day? I want marquisette! This is too stiff."

"All right, we will change it," the designer says, "but this is marquisette."

"What is marquisette in English?" Balanchine asks Farrell.

"Marquisette."

A seamstress spreads out the top layer of point d'esprit over the offending lower layers.

"I want something soft."

"Rayon?" the head seamstress pipes up in a little voice.

"Rayon!? We have never, never, ever used rayon," says Balanchine, feigning shock by staggering backwards. She slinks out the door.

"We need silk. Silk organdy."

"Organza," Ter-Arutunian corrects.

"Yes, that's right. Silk organza."

"And this velvet is no good. It is too thick," says Balanchine, pointing to the one-and-a-half-inch-wide strip of black velvet that trims the edge of the delicate top layer of point d'esprit.

"We need silk. Pure French silk ribbon."

The designer nods.

"Do you have?" Balanchine asks a seamstress.

"Shiny or plain?"

"Like this," he says, touching the bodice of the tutu.

"Satin. Yes, of course," and leaves to find some in the black ribbon drawer.

A large bolt of silk organza is brought in. Balanchine unrolls it and caresses it, smiling and spreading his arms. A roll of ribbon is produced.

"Can we take this off?" asks Balanchine, tugging slightly at the black velvet.

"Yes, of course. It is only basted," says a seamstress, instantly producing a pair of scissors before kneeling and snipping at the connecting threads.

The head seamstress enters with a pale blue costume that has a silk organza tutu.

"What is this?" Balanchine asks.

"It is Farrell's," she states, more strongly than before.

"From where?"

"From *Le Baiser de la Fée.*"

Balanchine looks surprised.

"Yes," says Farrell, "I never learned the steps." But the costume had been produced for the role, recently revised for the ballerina Patricia McBride. "Le Baiser de la Fée" was Stravinsky's homage to Tchaikovsky, just as "Mozartiana" was Tchaikovsky's to Mozart.

"But that is what I want. Like that," Balanchine says, pointing to the many lace-trimmed underlayers of silk organza with silk ribbons running through.

The head seamstress beams.

The velvet strip is off. Three seamstresses baste on the thinner satin ribbon and pin on black satin puff sleeves. The designer pinches one ball of material at Farrell's shoulder where he wants a smaller look; instantly a pin is applied.

As another woman places heavy white lace along the neckline, which Ter-Arutunian extends to the top of the sleeves, Balanchine interrupts, "That is no good. What is that?"

"This is the trimming on the costumes you sent us."

Balanchine fiddles with it pushing it down under Farrell's neckline until less shows. It still looks too bulky. "It is pretty, but no good."

The ribbon is basted around the hem of the tutu, and everyone approves. Balanchine asks Farrell to get out of the first tutu skirt and step into the *Le Baiser de la Fée* skirt.

"But leave the top, please." The sheer black layer is separated from the stiff marquisette and attached ruffled panties.

Farrell undresses to her leotard and steps into the *Baiser* skirt. The softer effect is perfect. She twists her hips as before and all the layers shift together. The underskirt is shorter and although it does not have the same bell shape, the quality is right. When the satin trim is removed Balanchine tugs, trying to lengthen the look of the underlayers. But Farrell surreptitiously pushes them up under the bodice, fulfilling his desire for even lengths yet keeping them as short as she wanted.

"This might make a difference," the ballerina says, stepping out of her shoes. It lowers the viewing angle. Balanchine makes no further attempt to lengthen her skirt. But he still looks perplexed and dissatisfied. The skirt is drooping; it isn't the look that either man originally wanted. But any more ruffles will look too thick. Balanchine sniffs. Ter-Arutunian arches his neck. Eventually a seamstress points out that with more ruffles higher on the hip and under the top layer they will get the bell shape they want.

Balanchine asks Farrell to lift her leg. The look is right.

"Her whole knee should show," Balanchine announces.

A date is set for next Wednesday. It will take four days to make the needed adjustments. Amazingly there seems to be plenty of time left for Farrell's costume. After Wednesday, there is another week before the gala performance. But costumes had been known to arrive only minutes before curtain, with mounds of material being sewn together, piece by piece, just before a performer's entrance.

LAST TWELVE BARS

———————— ⁌⁊ ————————

Balanchine is dressed impeccably at rehearsal on Tuesday. Instead of his white moccasins, he is wearing new shoes that match his tan trousers. His hair is perfectly combed. He sits rigidly watching his dancers run through their parts. No matter how many mistakes they make, he does not respond. The dancers in the Hungarian ballet struggle, wanting corrections, but he remains absolutely still. After a chance meeting on the street last week, he had invited the photographer Arthur Elgort to rehearsals. Photographs were needed for publicity. During this entire period, he had refused to let anyone shoot him or his new ballets. Naturally the photographer was elated at the privilege, but he had expected the usually mobile choreographer to make a more interesting subject. But Balanchine still poses. Not until the dancers finish the finale of the Hungarian ballet does Balanchine move.

He does not like what he has concocted. But it had been like this all week for this ballet. The styles, dancers, music and atmosphere were extremely different from *Mozartiana*. It was remarkable that Balanchine could have finished most of one and started the other in the same afternoon last week. They were as much in contrast as the climate of the Tyrolean

Alps, where Sophie Mentor and Tchaikovsky probably wrote most of these Hungarian songs in her castle, to the warmth of the low-lying Caucacuses in southwestern Russia, where the composer wrote most of "Mozartiana." Balanchine's attitudes matched these moods. Making *Mozartiana* he seemed to be constantly having fun, happy to be working, enthusiastic, while during the Hungarian ballet, he was testy and had physically to work harder. Von Aroldingen and Lüders were learning more slowly than Farrell and Andersen. Consequently, the choreographer had to repeat himself many times, before going to the corps of four couples and showing them a totally different set of steps to the same music.

Compared to the individual qualities of "Mozartiana," with its spiritual *Preghiera*, sparkling *Gigue*, formal *Menuet*, romantic *Theme and Variations* and brisk *Finale*, the bastardized Hungarian folk songs were endlessly repetitious. The choreographer would have to find various distinctions within their monotony. However, he knew what he had given himself. For when he mentioned the musical program for the Tchaikovsky Festival to Robert Irving, Balanchine had said, referring to these Hungarian gypsy songs, "Why does all music have to be the best? Let's have some cheap restaurant music."

The previous Saturday night Balanchine had taken von Aroldingen and pianist Moredock to a Hungarian restaurant which had a band featuring a cimbalom. This Central European stringed instrument was used in these previously "undiscovered songs," and Balanchine had wanted the pianist to absorb its spirit. During the meal the band played one of the songs! However, the laughter shared then was now gone.

Elgort quietly leaves his chair as the choreographer once more painstakingly demonstrates, explains, reworks, and constructs, piece by piece, dance by dance, couple by couple. The photographer snaps at the pensive face, the articulate hands, the stooped shoulders and hanging head. He catches a

129

gesture, a quizzical look of a corps member, an understanding look of von Aroldingen's.

Suddenly Balanchine turns on his friend and stalks toward him. He yells, pronouncing that he cannot work with the photographer lurking about. Balanchine grasps his own throat and squeezes his body as he sinks halfway to the floor. "I thought it would be nice to photograph the ballet and the beautiful dancers, not an old man like me. Look there. THAT is what people want to see. I feel surrounded at every angle," Balanchine continues, imitating the photographer scurrying from place to place.

For the next hour, the last third of the previous Hungarian rehearsal is reworked. The assembly of one phrase of music was razed then rebuilt, measure by measure. Nothing was kept, not even a pattern. Balanchine got the confidence to do this fifty years ago when he choreographed *Apollo*. "It was," he said, "the turning point in my life. In its discipline and restraint, in its sustained oneness of tone and feeling, the score was a revelation. It seemed to tell me that I could, for the first time, dare not to use *all* my ideas; that I, too, could eliminate. I began to see how I could clarify, by limiting, by reducing what seemed to be a myriad possibilities to the one possibility that is inevitable."

He works now with total concentration all the way through and past the place of embarkation, hardly acknowledging Robert Irving's arrival.

By the time Balanchine flings the dancers into their final climax, Moredock races with them. However, the music does not seem to fit.

Abruptly Irving, who had been squirming in his chair, springs to the piano bench, and leans his great frame over the hapless pianist. Irving pounds out the phrase as he wants it to be played. Just as the dancers have rarely seen Balanchine yell, the sight of Irving's piqued intervention is also surprising.

There is nervous laughter. Within two minutes Balanchine reaches the end. The dancers applaud him. Among them all, there is relief and gratitude. It has taken fifteen gruelling hours to choreograph sixteen minutes.

The children of *Mozartiana* soon sprinkle in, followed by Farrell. Andersen straggles in a few minutes later. It has been discovered that the cause of his sickness is a severe ear infection. By the time the cast of *Mozartiana* is ready, Balanchine is leaning back in his chair for the first time in a long while. "All right, can we do from beginning, please," he suggests. "We will do with Robert." The conductor sits ready to cue the dancers at Balanchine's direction. Richardson collects the children, and the photographer, having survived the earlier onslaught, settles into position, his camera ready for a discreet shot.

"Curtain up as music starts. Aaaand," Balanchine says, gesturing Farrell to enter with the little girls coming four beats later. Once again it is different than the last time when he wanted them to stand in place as the curtain rises—before the music begins. Irving and Boelzner settle the tempo of the preliminary bars before Farrell matches the music's celestial pitch. Irving, in a rainbow of colors—pink shirt, green pants and blue sneakers, says to Castelli, "Now there are two silent beats that I shall give you before your own downbeat. Like this," giving two sharp quirks with his elbow before a longer one from his shoulder. He repeats, and the dancer and pianist wait through the two flicks and start.

The tempo is much brisker than the other day and the variation is danced with greater ease because of it. The four young women enter on Castelli's last phrase and catch the conductor's beat as he once more stands in the center of the front wall by Balanchine.

Elgort snaps pictures of the two men in profile. Balanchine sits majestically, his head held high looking down his nose—this is usually his expression when he watches dancers dance.

131

It shows his respect yet at the same time it makes a dancer strive to impress him and break the judging facade into delight. But closer observation reveals the position comes as much from the need to take in the full scope of space and the dancer's relationship to it. With his head angled back and his eyes under half-closed lids, he has a more encompassing range. He is not haughty, as was sometimes thought; he is doing his job. The four women have passed his scan by dancing flawlessly.

"You start and they will enter," he tells Irving at the end of the *menuet* and before the principal couple promenades in like courtiers. The choreographer cues Irving and Irving cues both music and dancers with as few musical breaks as possible; though after Andersen's first variation and before Farrell's second, there is a change in mood strong enough to warrant a longer pause.

It has always been the policy of the New York City Ballet that the continuity of a performance should not be broken by applause. But if a stop lingers, it will certainly elicit applause from the audience, adding to the obvious discomfort of a break in continuity and concentration. Balanchine once said, "The theater is like a church; you don't applaud in the middle of a sermon or choral hymn." Applause is selfish on the part of the audience. By clapping, the audience is actually telling the performer to pay attention and is saying, "You see how nice I am to you. What are you going to do for me next?"

During the beginning of the *pas de deux*, as Farrell extends her limbs, ardently supported by Andersen, she silently mouths to Balanchine that it is too fast. Balanchine looks quizzically as if to say something to the two musicians. He feels the tempo for himself. It becomes stronger, more certain. He keeps quiet but evidently has realized something. The two dancers continue. In places they look very rushed, yet they manage all the way through, until the last twelve bars, when they stop and wait for the end to be set. Balanchine remains sitting. The conductor, who had turned to familiarize himself with the missing final pose, now waits. The dancers strike their last position. Elgort is poised.

"Finale," Balanchine announces. Farrell pauses, looks at him questioningly again, then exits with a "Shuffle Off to Buffalo."

Castelli and the children assume their positions on center.

"So I wait for Vicki and the kiddies to take their places?" quips Irving before giving the downbeat from his chair. The children miss it. The conductor walks to the center of the mirror, where they are used to seeing him. The finale splashes forward with waves of spritely children dancing to their master's imaginary baton.

At the end, Balanchine says a quiet thank-you, dismissing everyone. But he asks Farrell and Andersen to stay as Richardson takes the children downstairs to rehearse their parts for an hour. It would be their first *Mozartiana* rehearsal on their own. In the concluding minutes the principals work on the *pas de deux*, yet it still looks uncomfortable. Balanchine walks to the piano. The music stops. Farrell comes over.

"The *pas de deux* is too fast," she says matter-of-factly. The conductor rises to his full six-foot-four frame. Balanchine, realizes she has a valid point, interjects, "We made it very tight, the choreography. So the music must be exactly right. You did what the metronome says, but maybe we have to . . . I don't know . . . we have to look at it again."

The ballet master walks to the center holding the ballerina's hand. Andersen follows them. Irving sits down. The choreographer asks Farrell to take her last pose. She rises into *arabesque croisé* supported by Andersen. Balanchine steps in his place and takes one of Farrell's hands. He takes another and starts to turn her slowly. They dance it together to the piano until Balanchine kneels before her and she leans down with her head next to his as he holds both of her hands. Her leg extends straight up into the air.

Imitating an elderly man, Balanchine gets off his knee and asks Andersen to repeat the final sequence. Balanchine switches the dancer's knee. But he is not finished. He spends minutes working with the positions of both dancers' hands and Andersen's head until they are subtly framed.

They repeat the phrase once with the music. No corrections. Farrell leaves her final position with a warm smile. Balanchine is already smiling. Andersen stands to the side. The photographer takes a shot as Dunleavy enters the group. "So that's it," the assistant says with the widest smile of all.

He bows to his dancers and walks to the piano, taking Dunleavy with him. "You know, maybe . . . I think I will do a waltz for Tchaikovsky."

Dunleavy draws in her chin. "When?"

"Tomorrow."

He leaves, chuckling to himself.

FIRST
STAGE REHEARSAL
OF *MOZARTIANA*

———————— ⪧ ————————

The next day Balanchine does not make a waltz for Tchaikovsky, for there is no time. In the morning, the string section of the orchestra rehearses Tchaikovsky's Serenade for Strings in C Major, opus 48, the first waltz Balanchine ever choreographed for American dancers, and the sextet "Souvenir de Florence," opus 70, John Taras' choice for opening night after the gala performance. It is only the orchestra's second rehearsal for the Tchaikovsky Festival.

Most of the musicians know or have played the majority of the Tchaikovsky repertoire of the festival at one time or other in their careers. But still there seemed too few rehearsals. "Mozartiana" has been rehearsed only once and is scheduled to be rehearsed two more times before the premiere; once the day before and then the day of the gala. If a musician is unfamiliar with a work of music he is expected to practice at home.

After the orchestra has rehearsed and before the *Mozartiana* rehearsal begins, the asbestos fire curtain is raised. A rush of air hits the dancers' faces.

Boelzner walks along the footlights holding the metronome. He places it on the upright piano. The lunch break of the

135

stagehands is over and they work, avoiding the paths of the dancers. The children trail on, immediately looking out front, where their mothers sit waiting to see what they had only heard about. Fiorato and Balanchine appear simultaneously from opposite sides of the stage. Balanchine walks across to the piano, chats with the two musicians, then sits alone on the high stool center front with one foot on the floor, ready to rush and correct anything. The crowd of empty seats await.

"From beginning, please."

Farrell and the four young girls begin in the way decided on yesterday, with Farrell walking in as the music begins. Dara Adler and the other little girls follow four beats later.

"No good," says Balanchine, stopping the action. "If she enters there will be applause. When the curtain goes up, there will be applause," he announces in the conductor's direction before having the dancers take their places on center. The ballerina and the children rise and *bourrée* in place, shimmering.

"Like picture—still, like in a church," Balanchine says, holding up his hands in the shape of a halo and peering through. "Applause will stop and the music start. Ave Verrrruuummm," he hums, smiling. The beginning has been settled.

Before he starts to play, Boelzner warns the choreographer that only the first three dances were marked with the metronome. Balanchine's only response is to tap his foot silently at the metronome's speed, watching Farrell float over the stage. The children are visibly more assured. Last evening's separate rehearsal with Richardson has given them self-reliance.

After Richardson gives a few explanations to the children about the meaning of downstage and upstage, they encircle Farrell as she prays and glides to the church music. The mood is interrupted by the ungodly noise of stagehands unloading and storing the remaining scenery for the festival from two trailers offstage left.

The children exit and as Farrell leaves, Castelli races in from stage left to his place on center. He has timed the transition well. Fiorato gives him his two silent beats and starts the music in perfect style; he shines in his sleek, new unitard before finishing with a snap. Without a break the young women enter from their four corners.

Balanchine calls a halt. He decides that the quartet should *sauté* and stand, just as Castelli does the same jump and kneels. It was the same entrance step he had devised for the *menuet* dancers in his 1945 version. Castelli repeats his last sequence into the final step with the music, but Freedman misses her entrance. She tries again, but the sound of her toe shoes, a beat late, resonates into the vast space.

"Listen to the music," Balanchine insists; "there are eight chords. If you can't hear, dear, you will have to count and start on the sixth chord." She counts correctly and the *menuet* proceeds at an excellent tempo, giving the dance its full baroque qualities. The four women move unerringly until Freedman and Fedorova crash together. It is the same place that had given them difficulty when Balanchine choreographed it. It is an integral part of the design and he doesn't want to change it unless he has to. After a period of struggle, he gets his image.

The women leave by the closest wing as the lead couple enter upstage left from the fourth wing. Their choice of entry is acceptable, but they appear rushed. Some grandeur is lost. But Balanchine sits at peace, letting them finish the theme and begin their variations.

As they dance, they discover how their sequences fit in the width and depth of a different space here on the stage. When a dancer arrives on stage and the expanse increases, automatically his or her carriage of the chest broadens and the head lifts slightly. The eyes look deep into the blackness of the theater. Many dancers are intimidated by this change, but Andersen and Farrell have taken it over.

Andersen dances his multiple spinning variation better than ever. During the first series of slow *en dedans* turns in her second variation, Farrell looks uneasy. Balanchine claps. The music stops. Fiorato and Boelzner lean forward in their chairs. Ballerina and balletmaster look at one another. It is an impasse.

"What would you like?" Balanchine finally asks.

"Whatever you want," says Farrell, opening her hands.

"No, what do *you* want?"

"Well," she says, gathering her thoughts at the privilege of choice in a company where music usually rules, "it would be easier if it was a little slower." Balanchine faces the conductor and pianist, and says in a high nasal voice, pinching his thumb and forefinger together, "Maybe just a teeny weeny . . ."

"Hair," finishes Fiorato.

"A whisker," jokes Boelzner. The three men chuckle and the music resumes at a slightly slower tempo. Farrell fully extends the movements to their intended richness. Andersen's last variation is also danced impressively. The stage is giving their performances a new quality of perfection.

However, the third stop of the rehearsal is prompted by incorrect "spacing", the primary reason for the stage re-hearsals. It occurs at the end of the *pas de deux* when the dancers finish to the side of the dotted center line. Since the new sequence was assembled only yesterday, and separately from the *pas de deux*, the continuity caught the dancers by surprise.

Balanchine immediately takes Andersen's place next to Farrell. He walks a few steps diagonally forward toward center and starts to lead her around in yesterday's finish, but stops suddenly.

"Are you going to finish where you just finished?" he asks, referring to the pointe before the last twelve bars.

"Probably. Yes," says Farrell.

"So that's why we walk to center; have to end on center,"

he says, continuing as if he were strolling down a boulevard. "We'll do something," erasing yesterday's ending. Instead of walking around and kneeling before Farrell, with her leaning over his shoulder and raising her leg high, he takes her left hand with his right hand and slowly promenades around. He takes flat-footed steps as he leads her around back to back, careful to keep her on balance by creeping along an even circle. They stop with him closer to the audience. He asks her to lean on him. She lays backward across and over his shoulders, her leg lifted high.

"Come here, please," he asks Andersen, slipping out from underneath. Farrell remarkably remains on balance in a slow slung *arabesque* as the two men switch places.

With Andersen in position, Balanchine asks her to lean her head across her partner's shoulder. She stretches her long neck and raises her leg. Balanchine moves her face toward her partner's, steps back, then pushes her leg down until it is touching and following the length of Andersen's back leg. Her foot is barely off the floor. The ballet master raises her left hand held in Andersen's right. With their bodies molded together they make a long diagonal line.

"All right. Not so bad," says Balanchine of his understated ending with its low *arabesque*. "Going on."

Castelli and the children rush in together. He flashes down the center and the young dancers unhesitatingly dash to the footlights. The four women soon overtake them, then Farrell and Andersen overtake them all centerstage. The ballerina twirls in the frame of dancers who are dancing through patterns and combinations that catch all the color of the music. The excitement—controlled tension and alarm—is thrilling. In one hour Balanchine has made a whirling crystal filled with tenderness and passion. Yet it is only a rehearsal and the auditorium remains silent.

THE CHILDREN'S
REHEARSAL

Balanchine's silk scarf flutters over his blue blazer as he rushes into the changing room at Karinska's, visibly upset.

Farrell is in the center of the room in her redone tutu. Beautiful as it is, Balanchine does not look it over immediately. He paces around the room, stopping once to admire some simple Russian peasant-style shirts.

"What are these?"

"They're Jerry's for *Piano Pieces*," Ter-Arutunian says. The choreographer sniffs approvingly and roams the room once more before he begins to settle down.

"I just had two interviews," he says, "and do you know what both asked me? I bet you can't. The first question—each time!" He imitates a grating whine: "Why the Tchaikovsky Festival? Why do Tchaikovsky? They are like children that tug on their mother's dress and whine like this—why is the sky blue? That was my answer! Because. Because, why not? He is a great man. I have to DO. That is all. Now is the time! Why do they ask?" Many years ago he said of Stravinsky, "He was like Einstein—nobody like him. He made *musique dansante*. There have only been three who could do it. Delibes, Tchaikovsky and Stravinsky. They made music for the body

17A   David Richardson and Balanchine adjust Tamara Molina's hair while Amy Fixler and Lisa Cantor look on. Victoria Hall practices in the background.

B   Suzanne Farrell in the *preghiera* section of *Mozartiana*. From left to right: Tamara Molina, Lisa Cantor, Amy Fixler, and Dara Adler.

18A   Suzanne Farrell.

photo: © Carolyn George

photo: © Carolyn George   photo: Costas

18B&C   Suzanne Farrell and Ib Andersen in *pas de deux*.

photo: Martha Swope

9A Balanchine talking with, left to right, Nina Fedorova, Susan Freedman, Jerri Kumery and Suzanne Farrell.

photo: © Steven Caras

3 A *révérénce*. Left to right, Victoria Hall, Nina Fedorova, Jerri Kumery and Susan Freedman.

20A   Victor Castelli dancing the *gigue*.

20B   Suzanne Farrell

photo: Martha Swope

1A   Ib Andersen in *grand jeté en attitude*.

22A
Suzanne Farrell
waiting backstage.

22B
Amy Fixler
and Dara Adler
backstage.

George Balanchine

24 Lithograph created in 1956 by Christian Berard for a portfolio on *Mozartiana.*

to dance to. They invented the floor for the dancer to walk on." Balanchine glances at Farrell. Ter-Arutunian and a seamstress draw near. "Beautiful," he mutters.

"It's too long, don't you think?" she suggests. Balanchine steps back and looks. He bends down and looks. A signal is given and the seamstress immediately begins to tuck the yoke of the tutu up and under the bodice at the waist.

"Don't need this," says Balanchine, pointing to the two-inch-long bodice point extending down the center of the yoke covering her hips.

The choreographer flips up the layer of point d'esprit and studies the new underlying skirt, copied from the unused tutu of *Le Baiser de la Fée*. He runs his fingers over the four double ruffled layers of white silk organza. The seamstress smiles proudly.

"I think there is too much," he says. The tutu does not have the original bell shape. Two layers of double ruffles are carefully snipped off. Six yards of silk organza soon surround the ballerina's feet.

"Lift your leg, please," Balanchine asks. Farrell raises her right leg. Her bent knee reaches her shoulder. There is still too much material underneath. Another white ruffle billows softly to the floor.

By constant snipping, Barbara Karinska came to invent her famous tutu. Cutting off extra material from the long styles of the day, she costumed her first ballet—it was Balanchine's short-lived masterpiece *Cotillion*, which was designed by Christian Bérard. This was the ballet that convinced the young Lincoln Kirstein to work with Balanchine. It was danced by the 17-year-old Tamara Toumanova, and a year later she danced the first *Mozartiana*.

"I think the skirt should be blacker," interjects Ter-Arutunian. All the other female costumes are of solid black satin and velvet with no white except a lace neckline. "It should be a little closer to the look of the others," he concludes, and Balanchine nods. They ask for a swatch of point d'esprit to match the top layer of Farrell's tutu.

It is too black. "Maybe a finer point d'esprit."

The seamstress presents a finer version. "It feels like nylon," Balanchine says curling his lip.

She backs off horrified and is told at the doorway by another seamstress to find a different point d'esprit and cut fourteen inches to match the layer already atop the tutu.

The form-fitting bodice is fine but the neckline is too high. It is curled down into more of a scoop, just as Farrell predicted when she first tried the costume on.

"There is not much partnering. It will be all right," she says, referring to the low scoop and the dangers of having the partner hold the costume stationary while the ballerina bends backward with her bosom slipping out the top.

The black satin puff sleeves are replaced with puff sleeves of point d'esprit. Within a minute it is basted together. Balanchine picks up a piece of white ruffle off the floor and stuffs it under the new sleeves.

"No," says Ter-Arutunian.

Balanchine agrees, "Skin is better."

After the second layer of point d'esprit is presented, already sewn and shirred onto a string for easy, temporary use, the designer goes on to suggest there should be more lace on the neckline.

"No, it's like fur. We have a beautiful girl. . . . Only a tiny bit," says Balanchine.

As Ter-Arutunian instructs the seamstress about measurements and materials, Balanchine nods approvingly before leaving the dressing room. In the main room of the shop, however, he is interrupted by Sally Ann Parsons, the designer of the heavy matte jersey costumes for eight men in the *Pathétique*. He found the weight and movement perfect, especially when draped around Ter-Arutunian. Cramped for time,

Balanchine is forced to leave but reveals whimsically, "I am like a dog. I know only what I see."

Over the next two days, Balanchine assembles twenty children, sixteen couples, and nine other girls into a collage of flowers and floral patterns that blossom from one design into another like a kaleidoscope. Sixteen seven-foot pieces of stripped bamboo and nine lengths of three-foot rope, which will eventually be covered with flowers, are intertwined in this dance. Balanchine has chosen the Garland Waltz from the first act of *The Sleeping Beauty*, and works incredibly fast in the allotted four hours. As he begins, Balanchine says, "We are going to do it like it should be done. Not like some places where they have awful gray costumes like upholstery." He knew how it should be done because as a child he had performed in the original Petipa version with the Imperial Ballet. It brings back memories. He describes the "fountain girls" in the Imperial Ballet. They were the lowest echelon of the corps de ballet. The "firsts" could go on pointe and were paid higher than the "seconds," who were not as good; the "thirds" were the worst but the wealthiest. These girls danced in back by the fountains and rarely got a chance to be seen in front. They could barely stand on pointe. However they were the Tsar's beautiful mistresses. Most vividly Balanchine remembers their supported and bejweled breasts as they passed over him like a tray of sweets. The story provokes some dancers to make suggestive shapes with the pliable garland sticks. The childlike behavior alleviates boredom when Balanchine is concentrating on a group of dancers elsewhere. But the children act like adults.

These clusters of children in the Garland Waltz are within a larger group of children. In contrast, the four young girls in *Mozartiana* are apart from other children. They had been chosen from the crowd.

Downstairs in the lower concourse after one of the Garland

Waltz rehearsals, the girls in *Mozartiana* rehearse with David Richardson, who was once a little prince in *The Nutcracker*. He treats them, just as he had been, like adults and uses the same techniques as Dunleavy does in a company rehearsal. The space for a missing principal dancer is marked by an imaginary boundary, or is otherwise filled by Richardson himself. However, these little girls must always be aware of the girl in front of them and their counterpart across the stage. It takes years to combine the rules and still dance. Richardson concentrates instead on showing them the steps. These are not kiddie roles, as in the Garland Waltz, but demi-solo parts with four featured dancers and the central figure. Richardson asks one girl for more *épaulement* and stops to wait until she tilts her head enough to curve her neck, giving the finished quality of a mature dancer. He tells another, whose arms hit correct positions, to relax her elbows. They are transformed from scarecrow sticks into swan's wings. Another always tenses her hands too much. He has her soften them from claws to petals. When their shoulders rise as the steps get more difficult, Richardson's gentle voice soothes them down to their correct place. He shows them how to step boldly into position as though they owned the spot, not to take a million insecure "piddle steps." He shows them how to present their feet when stepping forward, exaggeratedly but graceful, allowing the audience, hundreds of feet away, to see them. Not a detail is missed as these children look more and more like miniature ballerinas. They forget their initial disappointment in not being allowed to wear toe shoes, for this was that special first year of wearing them. They sense Richardson's sincerity as he works them hard and polishes their technique. Their gained confidence shows. Many of the children have worked with him longer than new members of the company had worked with Balanchine.

Since they have performed in other ballets they are not afraid of opening night. It is almost like a privileged form of play now that they have learned their parts. But Richardson keeps them under control, for he knows the importance of their parts. This ballet is not like any other for children.

Four years studying at the School of American Ballet have given them their necessary technique and poise. Their look—well-proportioned and sinewy strong—shows the level that has been achieved by nearly fifty years of skimming off the best. What was essential were feet that will be strong enough to bear the severe demands of a career in pointe shoes yet look as delicate as Venetian glass; long necks, small heads with radiant faces and body structures that will likely evolve into even proportions. The school also takes the characteristics of the parents into consideration—if the mother is exceedingly heavy, there might be weight trouble and poor eating habits at home; or if both parents are short-limbed, perhaps the child will be. For the last five years the School of American Ballet has had the capacity for four hundred fifty students, from ages 8 through 20. The plan is to keep it that way and thereby develop even finer thoroughbreds. This intense competition has some bad effects at times, so Richardson tries not to be too harsh. Watching them whip off the combinations demonstrates the great strides that they, Richardson and the School of American Ballet have made.

TWO REQUESTS
FOR THE THEME
AND VARIATIONS

Suzanne Farrell's flowered shawl trails behind her as she crosses the back of the silent stage. Curled in a seat out front, an usherette is sleeping between a matinee and evening performance. The ballerina is on her way to a request rehearsal of *Mozartiana*. In the Main Hall, she and Andersen do a barre in the quiet room. The only sound is their feet brushing the floor as they stand at opposite ends of the studio. The sharper knock of Andersen's foot slapping the floor in *frappé* combines with the sliding sound of Farrell's *tendus*. Not until Boelzner arrives does the eccentric music stop. They take their places where the theme begins.

"I think we should let two beats go by, since we will have to start from the wings," Farrell states.

"It won't make any difference if you let a hundred beats go by. Behind all the plastic tubing you might not hear a thing," Boelzner says, raising a good point.

"Maybe we should come out and stand," suggests Andersen. Boelzner pounds a dissonant chord, a comment on this obvious conclusion. They dance the theme with the same ease as they did in the first rehearsals with Balanchine. The tempo is perfect. The first few variations also go rather well.

146

But Farrell seems on edge when a few dancers come in to warm up for performance. Sometimes she has felt that even the pianist is an intrusion on her privacy at a request rehearsal.

Violinist Lamar Alsop, also requested, arrives on time for the *pas de deux*. The main reason for this rehearsal is to test the timing of the dancing to the spontaneous violin breaks.

The concertmaster is ready to play freely. At first, the breaks are longer than Farrell expected. She dances on, falling short, but now knowing what to expect of herself and of the music, although many of the abrupt bursts seem to surprise her. The notes fall on specific steps she would not normally dance with Alsop's accents. But this is exactly what she wants to find out. Since Farrell is musically sensitive, she finds this a challenge. Her unique performances stem from her spontaneous responses to how the music is played at particular instances. Freshness and variety are inevitable with this ballerina.

The choreography dictates that Farrell break from Andersen just as the violin breaks from the orchestra. Farrell finds one break amusing, when Alsop innocently bows a double-stringed chord from G to E sharp. She laughs in mid-step. On most of the other breaks, the timing is altered just enough to make the steps feel more uncomfortable than before. The dancers keep up, but they are often unsynchronized. Not until the end of the *pas de deux* does Farrell speak up.

"We are going to need a little more time there," she says, referring to the double *pirouette penché* turn combination which cannot have been danced more correctly, yet still finishes too late.

Alsop amicably complies and stretches out the last note with a longer draw of his bow. It works, and they start on the finale and dance straight through. Although the rehearsal has been rough, Farrell and Andersen do not go back again. They are more concerned with seeing exactly how much the violin would alter their timing, learning how much more they would have to retain for the orchestra rehearsal the following week.

On Sunday, Andersen asked for another rehearsal for himself and his partner. Their performances in the first ballet of today's matinee were over. The rest of the company was still dancing the next-to-the-last program before the Tchaikovsky Festival. Starting with the theme, they work straight through but stop briefly in the middle of the *pas de deux*. Even then, the step that caused trouble is not repeated. Today stamina and continuity are their primary concern. Yesterday's difficult rehearsal is only an unpleasant memory. Andersen's main worry now is why he failed at both sets of his turns.

Hearing the heavy panting of the dancers, Boelzner tries to reassure them that there will probably be more time in between the variations than he is now taking, because the conductor will have to wait for the applause to fade after each variation so that the delicate instrumentation can be heard. Jokingly, Farrell tells Andersen that she will enter and strike such a glorious pose during his *pirouettes* that no one will notice if he falls off them or not.

However, their deepest concern surfaces. It is the tempos; Alsop's version and also the quicker time taken in the recording by Antal Dorati which Farrell has been listening to is unsettling. Andersen has listened also and agrees. But Boelzner is consoling, saying that Irving will have no trouble with that problem, an allusion to the conductor's generally brisk tempos.

Andersen asks Farrell afterward if she would like to review anything. She declines.

"In the variations, you think you're getting tired," she tells him, "but you're not. It is the middle of the *pas de deux* that is the most tiring place in the ballet." He agrees with her about the middle of the *pas de deux*. Yet he still felt his first variation is the toughest and adds that fluorescent lights bother him. Like Farrell, he feels the rehearsal studio, with its mirror, is now a hindrance; the fraction of a second a dancer keeps on his image is gained back on the stage.

STAGE
REHEARSAL

───────────── ✌୬ ─────────────

Balanchine visits the stage Monday, the company's free
day. The repertory season's assortment of painted drops and
colored scrims have been lowered, crated and stored in the
cellar three levels below the street. He wants to see the set
which was first a quick pencil sketch he had given to production stage manager Ronald Bates in December, when Balanchine and Lincoln Kirstein's Harvard classmate, architect
Philip Johnson, had talked about the idea of a crystalline
cathedral.

After weeks of deliberations, Johnson & Burgee Architects
delivered to Bates a scale model one half inch to the foot and
the designs were handed over to Sander and Gossard and
Associates Scenic Design Studio. They spent five weeks making six miles of one-quarter-inch-thick plastic tubing, two
weeks making galvanized steel trestles and aluminum connec-
tions. Twenty minutes were required to record all the technical information on their computer.

Balanchine notices that the original flat portals bordering
the sides of the stage have been replaced by a triangular
tower of galvanized steel divided horizontally into four sec-

tions with three platforms. Eventually the front of the forty-five-foot-high structure is covered in black velvet to match the overhead trim as with the previous portals. These are able to accommodate many extra lights on each platform and part of the auxiliary lighting system planned for his monolithic set design. It appears that the shop has altered a particular element of the design for logistical reasons. Balanchine expresses concern about one of the three steel supports that narrow the space in the first wing. The entrances of his dancers will be hindered, and their dashing exits with lights glaring in their eyes, quite dangerous. The only choice is to pad the metal support like a football goalpost.

Although Balanchine made a new architectural design for the Festival, he did not imagine that the designs would be structured to last for eternity. It was similar to the time when Balanchine asked for scenery simulating a house and a house was built for him. He complained, "Can I live in it? Can I rent it? Can I sell it? All I wanted was a little muslin and wood."

Historically, theatrical sets have been deceptively light and easily assembled and quickly dismantled. It is not the case for these sets. Bates and everyone working know that the galvanized steel trusses chained to the theater's overhead pipes, form a clumsy structure for hanging plastic tubing. However, Johnson & Burgee are not set designers—and the model did look stunning. As the stagehands start to chain a second truss onto two lowered pipes, Balanchine leaves. There are still a million things to do.

But by three o'clock Tuesday, Balanchine is forced to cancel all stage rehearsals. The stagehands, who have worked all day Monday and started at eight this morning, are discovering they have come up against an incredibly difficult hang job. Not until today do they realize how painstaking their task is. The design requires one hundred forty-eight different sizes of tubings ranging in length from six-and-a-quarter inches to ten-foot-nine inches. These one-half-foot diameter seamless wonders, with little holes drilled in both ends to allow for attachment to one another, have been unloaded from the three trailer trucks over the last three weeks. They have been stored in every available inch of backstage space—and smell horrendous. The stage crew sorted through the thirty-six thousand pieces of the transparent tubes to match the design exactly. These rows of lines of tubing are to be formed into arches, slants, and long horizontals. By now, only one wall of tubing is complete. But through all these troubles there looms an incalculable mystery.

It is weight. The weight of the "special" lights; the weight of the steel trusses; the weight of the six miles of heavy plastic tubing, added to the weight of the standard lighting, wiring and pipes already up. All that weight has to be counterbalanced to raise, lower and hang the set properly. Bates already knows he will have to make a concession to the design, for the theater's construction does not allow for as much counterweight downstage as it does upstage, and the design calls for many downstage tubes. This, the third largest theater in New York City has to send out an emergency call to theatrical suppliers and Broadway houses for at least six more tons of counterweights.

As it is, the stage will take an hour to clear. Calculating how much time has already been needed to accomplish so little, not one minute can be spared.

Rehearsals that desperately need stage space had to be put in various studios within the theater, the school and a ballet studio in a warehouse across the street. The work of other choreographers was also being disrupted.

In the Main Hall, before the rehearsal for the Garland Waltz, Balanchine is dancing a little soft-shoe shuffle before the smiling Susan Freedman and Jerri Kumery. He is singing a song he recently composed. Interrupting his fun, Dunleavy drags him away to start the rehearsal. John Taras is also here, free to keep an eye on the proceedings. The sixteen seven-inch sticks of stripped bamboo are now garlands. The property department has wired hundreds of silk and plastic flowers around them. But it soon is discovered that the flowers are too heavy for the strips of wood. The rehearsal is halted. The thousands of flowers will have to be taken off, another set of strips acquired and taped together for double strength—every single flower will have to be rewired. Dollies loaded with weights lumbered through rehearsal all afternoon. And Balanchine looked like a circus performer, racing to keep all his plates twirling on a stick, as he constantly revised one cluster or one design within the dance.

Mozartiana immediately follows the Garland Waltz rehearsal. Boelzner replaces Moredock at the piano and lays out the music. It is the first time Balanchine has seen *Mozartiana* in six days.

Designer Sally Parsons arrives through a crowd of parents and exiting dancers. Ter-Arutunian and Kermit Love greet her and disappear out the back door. They have left their costume samples out in the hallway. Lately, they have come to most every Balanchine rehearsal as different costumes from the yet unchoreographed *Pathétique* are completed. The designers know of the rehearsal of *Mozartiana* and question whether or not they should come back to show more costumes to him. The music starts and Balanchine says with a smile, "It's okay. I can do two things at once." An apprentice shyly floats in modeling a tan chiffon robe. Balanchine quickly approves. Love spots Kumery and leads her to the costumes in the hallway.

Farrell dances among the four little girls. For the first time all day the theater is calm; the ballerina is soothing. During the *gigue*, Kumery appears dressed as an angel, complete with ten-foot-high wings. Everyone stops and admires her. But when Castelli starts up again, he lands on the side of his foot.

He rises tentatively. He hears a crack. Balanchine blames the legwarmers, though Castelli has cut out stirrups to fit neatly over his ballet shoes.

"You don't need them. It's like fur," Balanchine says. But probably he fell from fatigue; for it is usually on the little steps, dancing quickly, that a dancer hurts himself; on high-flying jumps subconsciously he pays more attention to his landings. Dunleavy is already calculating that Castelli has three other ballets in the festival which he is to dance this week. He takes a few steps. At least he can put weight on it. Dunleavy mutters the old ballet adage that isn't necessarily true: If you can walk, you can dance. A former ballet mistress used to cure girls by telling them when they complained that their feet hurt, "If you can't dance, kick your toes against the wall until they're numb." The solution for Castelli now is a visit to Marika Molnar's office for an ice pack and diagnosis, and if serious, a visit to the company's orthopedic surgeon, Dr. William Hamilton.

The *gigue* has started again with Christopher d'Amboise replacing Castelli, even before the injured dancer is out the door.

With the start of the *menuet* Kumery is still in Kermit Love's angel costume. The company hairdresser is pinning her hair tightly so that a gold wig will fit over it without any lumps.

After Balanchine complains briefly to the designers, the *menuet* is started anyway. Balanchine slouches in his chair, he is uninterested because a part of his picture is missing. Yet the three bodies maintain a design because the combinations are true to every facet of the music. The dance corresponds to the construction of the musical form, rather than simply duplicating its line and beat. If it did, it would probably be boring and merely pretty.

KABOOM. The freight elevators open and more weights are wheeled across the room, breaking up the continuity of

Andersen's and Farrell's variations. However, their *pas de deux* shows signs of their work over the weekend. It is well timed. The ballerina keeps her serenity. Balanchine softens a bit in his chair.

D'Amboise and the four children charge forward at the start of the finale, only three big girls return and interchange with the four little ones, Andersen and Farrell return and join the ensemble. Castelli returns, looking more serious. He is walking slowly. Anyone else probably would have broken their foot, but his thin ligaments allowed more flexibility. If they had been torn, he wouldn't be walking.

Balanchine is watching d'Amboise and guiding him to the right positions as the finale continues to its brief swirling finish.

The choreographer rises and changes the end of the *pas de deux*, now that he has seen his ballet from a more objective view. Instead of a slow promenade into the final low *arabesque* pose, he has Andersen and Farrell hold hands and step away then toward each other—a formal *menuet* under arched arms, before they take the same formal pose with half a promenade.

Balanchine retraces his work mentally and comes upon a new idea. He leads Andersen away from Farrell and changes a step in his first variation.

"Instead of *jeté*, you do this," he says, jumping into a surprise scissoring twist in the air. Andersen looks dumfounded. Balanchine twinkles. Farrell smiles, acknowledging his agility. Andersen attempts the interesting *grand jeté croisé fouetté effacé failli en l'air*. Balanchine shows Andersen again. It is a step the Danish dancer has never seen. Robbins has used it for years. Andersen does the step on his next try. It fits perfectly into his clockwise half circle, cutting the corner and allowing an added fraction of time to finish his variation, for he will land on the opposite foot, thereby cutting an extra step in preparation for the finish.

The *Mozartiana* dancers are dismissed, and Peter Martins starts immediately on one of his new ballets.

While Martins' leading dancers, Sean Lavery and Darci Kistler, dance through a sweeping corps de ballet to the second movement of Tchaikovsky's first symphony, Balanchine walks to the back where the angel, Jerri Kumery, still waits. He approaches her and admires the wings. They are curved, just as Love has promised. Ter-Arutunian suggests that the white unitard, underneath the white chiffon robe, be dyed a shade of tan. "The body will be seen underneath the white robe," the designer explains.

"Yes," agrees Balanchine, "otherwise, she looks like a bottle of milk."

THE DAY
BEFORE

─────────────── ෭ ───────────────

The stage crew returns at eleven o'clock that night, just after rehearsals finish. They work until four-thirty in the morning and return only four hours later that same morning. On this, their third straight day of work, the set still is not hung. Bates knows now that it is going to be almost impossible to finish on time. Not one lighting cue for the whole festival has yet been made. The lights can't be set until the scenery is up. No one has even tried to light six miles of tubing before. Specific cues cannot be made, written and distributed until the costume rehearsals are held onstage. Over the past weeks, only general ideas have been figured out as Bates has listened to tapes of the music. The dancers have early use of the stage today.

Tomorrow is the gala opening.

Jerome Robbins is rearranging *Piano Pieces* while Jacques d'Amboise is having trouble with one of his three ballets. The last movement of Tchaikovsky's famous never-ending endings was draining his imagination. Peter Martins is frantically replacing Castelli in one of his new works. John Taras continues ad-libbing with unscheduled works having assumed responsibility for others' unfulfilled assignments, and poor Joseph Duell has been allowed to develop only one of his ideas.

Today, before Farrell's *Mozartiana* rehearsal, she and Martins have a typically brief request rehearsal with their usual fun. It was for the *pas de deux* from Tchaikovsky's Piano Concerto No. 2, a ballet which Balanchine first choreographed in 1941 for American Ballet Caravan on its tour to South America. It was called *Ballet Imperial*, and had a beautiful set, painted to match the same shades of turquoise, gold and silver of the Maryinsky Theater. It depicted an embankment and bridge outside the Winter Palace along the Neva River in St. Petersburg. But Balanchine, as with many of his ballets, calls it now by its musical name, for he says: "Nothing is imperial any more—only the Hotel Empire," referring whimsically to the tourist–class hotel across from Lincoln Center.

Briefly, the festival seems ages away as the company's reigning king and queen act like court jesters alone in the Main Hall. Boelzner plays the great sprints up and down the length of the keyboard, with the two principal dancers dancing with all their regal confidence. Martins, in his variation, barely thirty bars of music, begins to slough off. When Boelzner asks if he wants to dance his variation through once more, Martins jokes, "What variation?" but he does dance it. On his repeat, Farrell teases him about changing the choreography and simplifying what little there is.

Marking through their *pas de deux*, they let everything go. Becoming more and more off balance, they end on the floor, in an unimperial heap, laughing. Other times, they spoof the virtuoso concert circuit classics with her holding her balance by herself and purposely keeping her partner waiting, totally disregarding the music for the adulation. Keeping up their "performance," Martins imitates Irving conducting during her variation. He picks up the speed, and Boelzner follows the beat.

"Slower, Gordon, please," says Farrell, now concentrating on herself in the mirror. Martins pumps faster. Farrell's eyes dart to the pianist. The music is becoming impossible. The ballerina yells out again as she keeps pace. The music is finally ridiculous. She breaks her concentration and glares at the source. Martins' chest swells like a pigeon's with his arms flapping faster as Boelzner shakes with laughter. Farrell twirls into hysterics.

There are no real problems with this ballet; Farrell and Martins have performed it many times together. Sobering up, she gathers a new set of toe shoes and hurries down to *Mozartiana* onstage. As she goes Martins says, "I love rehearsing with Suzanne. It's never like a rehearsal."

As Farrell arrives onstage, she finds the tension of the imminent opening. Andersen is drenched from previous rehearsals. Christopher d'Amboise is not grinning; he will have to perform the *gigue* tomorrow. With concentration he is mentally shaping his steps. His father, Jacques, sits downstage near the footlights, among other dancers waiting to watch Balanchine's new ballet. His mother, an ex-soloist, now a photographer, Carolyn George, gets in position to take pictures. In the opposite corner of the stage Robbins waits for his first view of *Mozartiana*.

The children are on their feet, jumpy with anxiety. Out front in the audience, among dancers waiting to rehearse, their mothers try to sit calmly. One dancer has folded down four seats and is napping in bent angles around the armrests. Also in attendance are John Corry and Hubert Saal. Balanchine takes his seat on the high stool downstage center. His back is straight.

Boelzner starts. The music rises to the chandelier. Balanchine remains still. The *Preghiera* glides wonderfully. Somehow Farrell has the same assurance she has had in her previous rehearsal, and the children dance with complete grace, leaving Richardson with little to correct.

After taking centerstage, d'Amboise gets confused in a number of places and wants to stop. Balanchine lets all the mistakes go by and signals for the *menuet*. Apprehensive about the apparent lack of concern, d'Amboise confers quietly with Dunleavy.

Balanchine's only request during the following dance is that his long-limbed women bend their bodies more. He rises only once during the theme.

"No one can see this, or this, or ANYTHING," he says, raising his voice and miming the interchanging arm gestures that pass between the dancers. The ballet continues, slower, Andersen has regained his strength from the dizzy spells caused by his ear infection and Farrell remains flawless. Both are amazed at how "on" they are.

Apparently, Boelzner has gradually raised the tempo, for by the end of the *pas de deux*, though the dancers manage gracefully, the tricky double *pirouette* behind the back grasp *arabesque penché* swing into the triple *pirouette posé* is rushed. Balanchine, however, makes no comment and the finale bursts forth with d'Amboise managing a smile as the children dance for their parents.

Not until the end does Balanchine change a combination; it is for the two male dancers in the back, when Farrell is dancing within a semicircle of the corps. What has been a series of *pirouettes* and changed to a series of jumping *entrechat six* are now changed to *sautés passés*. The movement is an extension into the air of the position the women are dancing on pointe in front of them and which Farrell was turning in. His change gives the appearance of terraced layers.

During the final pose, Balanchine fiddles with the children and has them kneel closer to Farrell instead of stretching the rear line of four women. They are no longer lost from view. He adjusts their heads and arms individually, thanks everyone, and fumbles for Farrell's hand. Together they stand still as everyone moves on to another rehearsal.

Dunleavy excuses all the dancers but d'Amboise and interrupts Balanchine. "I have to wait until he learns; then I will show him how," Balanchine replies. As he turns, Farrell asks him if he would like to see the costume. He nods, and she disappears to her dressing room. As Balanchine waits, Robbins expounds in earnest, "It is marvelous. Beautiful. It is so witty and fascinating. The variations, so light . . . each one." He stops short, at a loss for words. In the pause, Balanchine and Robbins share each other's warmth silently.

"So it is not at all like the old one," Robbins says, collecting himself.

"Absolutely. It would be impossible." Each one had been for a particular ballerina at a particular time in his life—Tamara Toumanova, Holly Howard, Alexandra Danilova, and now Suzanne Farrell.

In her new costume, Farrell returns to the stage to dance the finale again with Andersen. The costume moves satisfactorily. But Balanchine thinks the black over the white might be too thick, until realizing that nothing can be determined without the correct stage lighting. Late tonight they will have to return when Bates is here and the lights can be used. Another girl will be called in to wear the costume because he wants Farrell to rest. She protests, but Balanchine insists.

The focus now switches to d'Amboise. The gutsy dancer takes his place on center stage. Balanchine stands above his father and watches what the young man has learned.

"Pick up your feet higher," he calls out. The dancer tries, but does not get the desired effect. Rising from the floor his father shows exactly what he thinks Balanchine means. The son smiles at his father's sincerity as Jacques prances in a circle showing the correct size *emboîtés*. His mother snaps a picture. The young dancer follows his father's footsteps literally.

"That's right!" exclaims Balanchine as he leaves immediately for the fifth floor.

161

The cast of the waltz has waited for ten minutes. The unflowered garlands lie on the piano. The front door is stuffed with parents looking on and a few board members sit with Balanchine's assistant Barbara Horgan. Jennifer Dunning of *The New York Times* has the air of innocence that a journalist exudes unintentionally when covering a beloved place, while the photographer, Costas, sits quietly in the corner. Near the piano is the pontifical Mme Lucia Davidova, a White Russian who met Balanchine on the first day he arrived from Europe. She has remained a friend of his for nearly fifty years and is respected by all dancers who have come before her pleasant if imperious manner. Balanchine acknowledges her formally, and in response she inclines forward, as if her metal folding chair were a golden throne.

The music is resplendent, drawing full smiles from the newcomers. The dancers bend to four vamps and move forward; it is as if sunshine has broken over the audience. On the second wave of waltzes, Balanchine mutters to Dunleavy, then wades into the children. He changes a step and the direction of their combination. Except for one little girl all respond perfectly. She is asked to repeat it within her own small cluster but keeps dancing it wrong. The step is explained again and all are asked to dance. Although Balanchine watches the little girl out of the corner of his eyes, she dances as if he was staring at her. The music stops. In a very gentle voice, Balanchine asks her to dance it alone. Mme Davidova smiles protectively at the frightened little girl as if she were her own granddaughter. The child is unaware of Davidova's sympathy as she struggles on. On the sixth try, Dunleavy dances the combination slowly in front of her. Although she feels everyone watching, the little girl makes one final attempt.

"That's right!" Balanchine whoops, and the little girl reels back to her companions. She is blushing. For the first time she has heard those magic words of Balanchine's.

As the dancers proceed, Balanchine repairs a dead spot where the men had stood on the side with their garlands overhead. Like a gardener, he brings the flowers to life by looping the garlands over the ballerinas as their legs shoot straight up in the air in an *arabesque penché*. The dancers wave their arms to the waltzing rhythm.

It is as though a story Balanchine had once told her has materialized: the critic Clive Barnes once wrote how awful the *port de bras* of the company was. He said that the New York City Ballet dancers jutted out their arms at all angles with no sense of unison whatsoever. At their best, he said, their arms did not compare with those of the Royal Ballet. Balanchine explained Barnes' quotation: "Well, you see, Clive Barnes is English—and in England, all their gardens are trimmed. They are beautiful, but they are cut . . . short . . . shaped into formal, tight designs. Whereas in Russia, we have great open fields of waving flowers."

When the end is reworked and finished, Balanchine leaves the ballet to Dunleavy. She assumes her usual place during large rehearsals, on top of a chair by the mirror and directs the dancers to start from the beginning. Her task is to work through a myriad of minor discrepancies and clean up the ballet.

After roaming into other choreographers' rehearsals, to give pointers and encouragement, Balanchine returns to the Main Hall for his rehearsal for *Hungarian Gypsy Airs*. A few dancers are missing. It is the first time this season, in any of his new ballets. His rehearsals always receive priority by the dancers. But due to emergencies, the missing dancers are replaced by Garielle Whittle and a new understudy, Victoria Hall, who has proven in *Mozartiana* that she is most dependable.

Von Aroldingen and Lüders who have three more hours to work, extending long into the night, want to take it easy. *Hungarian Gypsy Airs* is not scheduled until the second week of the festival. Balanchine races through it, not rising from his chair to pick apart and patch as he has done all day long to his completed ballets. The rehearsal is repeated when two female dancers return from another rehearsal which had run overtime. A common occurrence now.

Again and again, Balanchine runs over his most troublesome ballet. Finally he wants his dancers only to walk through and mark its tempo. When Balanchine leaves, they collapse. But he returns shortly with his metronome and places it on the piano. Their drained faces gaze at the mechanical pyramid that will determine the speed. Since the first movement is marked *andante con moto*, Balanchine asks the pianist, "What does seventy-two sound like?" Moredock sets the metronome and plays the opening measures. Balanchine's face drops and the pianist stops playing.

"That's no good," says Balanchine. "You know why I asked for seventy-two?" Moredock does not answer. "Because it was Stravinsky's pulse!"

The pianist remarks, "Come to think, yes, much is written in seventy-two."

"Yes," says Balanchine, "he always checked his pulse before he wrote, and it was usually seventy-two beats a minute."

Regardless of this fact, they decide sixty-six is best for the opening; one hundred twenty for the allegro of Lüders and von Aroldingen, and one hundred forty-four for the finale.

That night, as the company tries to sleep before the opening gala, its collective heartbeat is probably one hundred eighty.

THE NIGHT
BEFORE

At one in the morning of June 4, Ronald Bates and his crew
have been at work for three hours. A small group stands in a
clearing as men stream on and off looking for tubes and attaching them. The apprentice who modeled the tan robe on
Tuesday, Edward Bigelow, Rouben Ter-Arutunian and Balanchine seem to be the only stationary beings in the theater.

Bates lingers near the huddle, giving Farrell's costume the
once-over on the sleek apprentice. Hovering around her, Ter-
Arutunian fluffs and tugs. The choreographer asks for a spotlight. Instantly a giant eye emerges from the semilit auditorium. The Farrell substitute, Sabrina Pillars, squints
momentarily looking into the one-hundred-eighty-five-foot-
long beam coming from above and behind the top balcony.
What was beautifully delicate at the costume shop is washed
out. The fine lace bordering the neckline fades into her white
skin. Bigelow excuses himself to Mme Pourmel's costume
room and soon returns with two different thicknesses of lace
and three different kinds of black ribbon. Balanchine chooses
a strand of lace which is similar to the original one. Ter-
Arutunian helps him place it around the neckline and sleeves,

as Bigelow serves as a ruddy seamstress with a fan of pins in his mouth.

Bates suggests a second spot. Balanchine nods. Two eyes stare down. Pillars now glows. Suddenly, she has the special color that only Farrell has on stage. The ballerina always looks much brighter and lighter than any other dancer, especially when dressed in her usual white. It seems that she has always had two Dynabeam spotlights focused on her; these modern Trouppé beams are an even more powerful combination. Balanchine fiddles with the yoke of the skirt. There is a space between it and the bodice causing a shadow. Heavy lace is placed over the difficult area. The balletmaster and designer inch around the proscenium and enter the auditorium for a better view.

"Kill the work lights and just give me the regular set," Bates yells out. The yellowish haze of lights is overtaken by the higher-watt stage lights. The plastic tubing picks up every splash, making a spectrum of angles. The stage has its normal complexion with Pillars standing on center. The lace around the neckline is good, but clumsy around the yoke. The thin, satin trim around the hem of the tutu doesn't seem strong enough to balance out the neck. Bigelow is directed to remove the lace of the yoke and places a thick trim of velvet ribbon over the satin strip. Balanchine and Ter-Arutunian agree on the look as Bigelow stands behind Pillars and lassos the ribbon over her head and around the hem.

Rushing back up to the stage, Balanchine and Ter-Arutunian scurry like two boys into a toy store, dabbling until they find something. Balanchine takes a strip of velvet, folds it in half, and runs it along a seam up the front of the bodice. The designer steps back and squints under his brows, deciding that the velvet strip be a third the width of the bottom trim. Finally, after Bigelow has placed the pins, Pillars is thanked by Balanchine.

"Wait. You're back," Ter-Arutunian calls to the dancer

way offstage. They catch up to her by the new floor sample which is much simpler and more satisfactory than the ones they had been testing. This one of interwoven slats was designed by Bates and stage manager Perry Silvey. Under the lamp of the nearby bulletin board, they all decide that a thin trim of velvet be placed along the top edge of the bodice of Farrell's costume for *Mozartiana*. Balanchine and company depart.

Since the end of rehearsals, the theater is like a ship in drydock. The stage is a deck full of activity. Ninety-nine lines of rigging are exposed, all the way past the catwalks. The borderings, wings of black velvet, are tied out of the way like sails lashed to a mast. Just above the seats of the orchestra, the brilliant chandelier has been lowered for cleaning. A crew of electricians are refitting its lamps while the property crew wipes off the dust and dirt. Work lights on the actual ceiling of the theater shine through a layer of steel mesh, revealing the skeletal network like the ribs of a hull.

A single steel truss has been lowered and half the carpenters hang strands of tubing, working horizontally, attaching one piece at a time to each strand. The pieces never end. With a representative of Sander & Gossard double-checking, stage manager Kevin Tyler calls out from his big book of design instructions, "On this row, give me four seven-by-elevens, six eight-by-sixes, six eight-by-tens, eight four-by-fives, two three-by-fours." The other half of the carpenters search for and eventually deliver this most recent order. The work is exacting and tedious.

After one and one-half hours, the time it takes to fill one hanging, John Walters, the master carpenter, yells up to the flyman, "Okay, Bob, take her out." The pair of pipes start to rise as one when Bob Ceplo and the rest of his strong corps haul at the corresponding lines. Like a clatter of giant wind chimes, the tubes are lifted.

The flymen, usually the size of bulls, man the catwalks,

unlock the lines and twist them together. At the same time they keep hundreds of pounds from falling and balance the weight of the scenery and counterweights. Fifteen tons of extra weights were received today, added to yesterday's six.

Near three o'clock, Bates asks Tyler to find the floral backdrop and "legs" from Lorca Massine's *Printemps* of nine years ago. Lincoln Kirstein had felt it would be best to cover the tubing for the first part of the gala opening—when the orchestra and singers will perform on stage—to save the architectural design from view until the ballets begin.

They couldn't be found in the office files, so Tyler went down, as instructed by Bates, to the cellar, to dig up the drops from *Vienna Waltzes*—high, wide panels which give the effect of ballroom mirrors. Four levels below the stage, the cellar holds crates packed with drops, scrims, dropweights and props from hundreds of ballets. They form mountains of ominous shapes in the dimness of this cavernous vault, which extends halfway under the theater. But Tyler knows his way and soon informs Bates that "there was only one leg in the dead box and one leg in the *Ballo de la Regina* box." They don't want to have to use and ruin new Mylar drops, for Bates wants to crinkle them to make the lights refract, but he also doesn't want the audience to recognize them as the mirrors of *Vienna Waltzes*. Crew members go down to find the missing two pairs of needed legs, which would hang along the side of the stage.

The atmosphere is tense with the growing realization of the enormous task. All had been working around the clock since Monday morning at eight o'clock; it is now past three on Thursday, and the set still isn't hung. The lights aren't set and not one cue has been made; at least four hundred tubes offstage right have not even been touched. Bates concedes he probably will not have the chance to use them by the opening gala. By four o'clock, Bates calls in the "electrics," and the carpenters catnap in the first place they find.

The entire lighting system will have to be refocused. These include five pipes of overhanging lamps, plus those on the bridge, the lighting from both sides behind the five sets of wings, in addition to all the front lighting in the ceiling and under the rims and tips of each balcony, plus the new specials. More new lights will also be attached and set to the new portal towers. They can only hope that the new light controls will work simultaneously with the theater's elaborate electrical control system that pays thirty thousand dollars a month to Con Edison.

The piano tuner arrives at his usual time of four-thirty and starts tuning the pit piano. The distinctive monotonous taps of a key repeat over and over and over.

A flyman is sitting in the front row as Bates checks the height of the black velvet horizontal portal framing the front of the stage. By cueing another flyman on a catwalk, they "trim" it at thirty-two feet, five inches; a height high enough for someone in the top balcony to see the whole stage yet low enough for someone in the front seats not to see the first row of overhanging lights.

His Arkansas twang is beginning to sound through his usual reserve, as Bates calls for the full backdrop of tubes to be hit by the last overhead pipe of lights. His face fills with amazement. The tubes bounce the light in a thousand directions—everyone hesitates and gazes at the spectacle. It is the first sign of what their work has produced. However, it does not affect the representative from Sander & Gossard, who is asleep.

Bates tries to balance the glistening tubes with lighting from the side. The special lights shooting down the tubes mixed with the standards make a concave and convex stalemate of dullness, and one or the other alone is not enough. All five hundred lights in the theater may have to be readjusted.

"Kill the work lights and give me everything, please." Blackness, and then a split-second surge of power sends

169

vibrations through the deck. Fissures of light splash over the icicle array. The stage manager and master electrician spend minutes making mental notes of their new environment before concentrating on the rear pipe of overheads. The others are turned off, yet the heat is still felt.

An electrician, Walter Kaiser, climbs onto the cherrypicker with an assortment of colored gels and a wrench. He waves good-bye as his little platform rises thirty-five feet above the deck.

Kaiser is told which light needs new gels and which unit needs adjustment; then exactly how much in order to produce the most glistening effect. Tyler has to record each differentiation from the standard set. For the altered lamps and colors will be changed back to their original positions after the festival. It is an extremely arduous process. Six long trips across the stage are needed. Kaiser is replaced after two hours, while Bates and Perry Silvey concentrate on focusing the many sidelights.

The carpenters return triumphantly from their cellar search. The rest of the Mylar has finally been found. Those who have been catnapping are awakened. An order to crumple the Mylar rings out from Bates as if from an Arkansas pig-farmer. The entire crew rolls up the long heavy panels and steps on it. They stomp on it; they dance on it. They take running flops like children into a pile of autumn leaves; they roll around and clown on it. But then the Mylar has to be hung with the crew standing in line tying the cords to the pipe. It gets caught on the now crowded rigging above. Painstaking and delicate maneuvering prevent it from tearing on the tubing.

Gels of blue and amber color the predawn. A pause is called at six-thirty a.m., before the pillars are secured to the deck with chains and a wooden block. The bridge lights are eventually brought into focus, and the house panel of electrical controls, behind the orchestra seats, comes into action as the front lights begin to be focused.

By eight o'clock the voices are softer. Only flat slaps of discarded gel frames and the sporadic clattering of plastic tubes are heard as the crew continues in a fog of slow-motion pantomime.

A clearer scale of notes comes through the din.

ORCHESTRA
AND
DRESS REHEARSAL

————————— ᶜᵉ⟩ —————————

Three hours later, at eleven, the dancers finish their class. It started at nine-thirty, the earliest ever for a company class. Farrell is already on her way to Karinska's shop to see if her costume now feels right. Somehow the crew is still standing. One member wakes up blind in one eye, then realizes he has dozed off into his breakfast. The deck has become a stage, covered with portable wooden platforms and completely trimmed to 80,000 cubic feet. Already the orchestra has been rehearsing for half an hour. Most of the musicians accustomed to playing in the pit, had never been on stage; now talented musicians and shrewd poker players will be shined up, restrung and set squinting into their well–earned spotlight.

They are very much at ease playing Tchaikovsky's *Romeo and Juliet* with melodious splendor. But there is a problem. Balanchine discovers that the sound is four times greater onstage than out front. All the music is going straight up the tubes. Balanchine, Bates, Irving and Fiorato decide not to use artificial amplification for this surprising lack of sound. The choreographer wonders if the back of the orchestra can be built up higher. Fiorato thinks that a stronger attack upon the instruments wouldn't be heard as a harsh tone but would produce the volume needed. To push the sound forward Bates promises he will hang the Mylar backdrop so it gives a ballooning effect that might push the sound forward. With so little time all that can be done is hope for the best.

The orchestra strikes an A and with piquance a soprano hums her aria from Tchaikovsky's *Pique Dame*, in harmony with Irving. The tenor, Howard Hensel, who is also with the City Opera, follows with Lensky's aria from *Eugene Onegin*. He appears to be in fine control and sings with power.

When the orchestra's rehearsal comes to an end, the crew strikes the podium, platform and music stands to clear the stage for the dancers while the orchestra returns to the pit. They look in wonder at the set. As usual, the company has only one orchestra and one costume rehearsal for each new ballet. Leaving his seat behind Bates' desk in the center of the orchestra seats, Balanchine returns to the stage for *Mozartiana*. He leans over the footlights to tell Irving softly, "Curtain rises and let them come out." Farrell and only three of the children take their places.

"We are ready," calls out the conductor. "Are you ready?" Dunleavy searches for the missing child. Balanchine motions to the conductor and the music gently begins. Farrell *bourrées*, looking to the far reaches of the house. Tenderly, the strings sing.

As Farrell floats by, dark-haired Tamara Molina dashes onstage. Balanchine goes to the children and places them equidistant from center before the final pose of the *Preghiera*. While Castelli, elegant with a plexiglass cane, stands in the wings, d'Amboise enters and keeps the tempo. Suddenly, the four women who dance the *menuet* charge out from behind the tubular wings, halfway through his *gigue*. They enter on the right notes but have forgotten about the repeat. Their giggles come as fast as the music. At least they entered together. If it had been a performance, all would have probably held their poses for the unknowing, possibly surprised audience.

They return correctly with their big *sauté pas de chat*, as Irving looks down to his left toward his cellos for the first strains of the *menuet*. By the time the violins enter four counts later, Balanchine asks the conductor to make it slower. The quartet dances smoothly and exits smoothly.

Farrell asks Balanchine if she and Andersen should start in the wings. "Let's see if you start there," he says, referring to the exact spot where they now stand. Irving gives his clear downbeat and the two dancers, for the first time sure of their entrance, walk with élan. Balanchine is conducting once again, though to himself, as Irving leads his orchestra at a leisurely pace.

Farrell dances her best performance in the first variation. Andersen smiles, buoyed by the music. In the beginning of Farrell's second variation, the delicate instrumentation is too faint for the ballerina to hear. Adjustments are made. The fourth variation goes untouched by Balanchine, although Andersen misses his turns and the tempo seems slower than ever before. Farrell asks for her following variation to be even slower, which gives her a chance to show off the steps that complement the interplay of cellos, violins and woodwinds. Musically, Andersen's last variation, the sixth of the theme, is the most interesting for it is accompanied only by the wind section. There is tartness in his playful bounding. Farrell returns with the strings, dancing her brief and final variation, before Andersen joins her and the full orchestra plays the rushing entrance of the quartet of young women.

Left alone with the sound of the solo violin, the couple draws together. Although the violin breaks seem a little too drawn out for the ballerina to sustain her movements, Balanchine does not seem to worry. The dancer is most concerned about the tempo, while the choreographer concentrates more on the musical shading's effect on his steps. He only asks for the lower notes of the violin to be bowed harder. Not pleased with the last measures when they are repeated, Irving states, "We need a dum plick pluck tium." Balanchine nods.

In the tenth variation, the brass section adds a gaudy sound. On Farrell's twirls around the stage, the principal clarinetist, David Weber, spins off on a cadenza. She stops but he keeps running. It is where she has always stopped. She starts up and chases the runaway clarinet, giving Irving a quizzical look. The conductor taps his baton on the podium.

"Thank you. That is plenty," he says as gales of laughter rise from the pit. Because the score doesn't give the length of the cadenza, the clarinetist played as long as he wanted to, relishing the solo. Choreographically, it worked out to be sixteen bars. Having just finished a *pas de deux* that had irregular breaks of the violin, Farrell was now going to have to be prepared for the ending of an ad-lib clarinet cadenza. A little deflated, she finishes exactly with the crash of a cymbal on her next try.

By the end of the rehearsal of *Mozartiana*, Barbara Horgan has come down from her office to join Balanchine and sits with him, giving the messages he has received. He can't afford to leave the rehearsals now.

The orchestra seats are now half full with dancers, columnists, photographers and television film crews. Ter-Arutunian, arriving from the costume shop, sits in a seat off to the side of Bates' desk in the center of the orchestra seats.

Bates, with his mike around his neck, gives continuous directions to the electricians who are still focusing and refocusing. The front lights along the back wall of the second balcony and the recessed portions of the ceiling are being reset. He has run up against many unfortunate problems lighting the set, even though tests were made months ago. Lighting a few tubes gave a different perspective than lighting thousands. The scale model, though made of the same plastic acrylic, had solid cylinders as opposed to hollow tubes. Consequently all previous lighting plans made during the interim and tried on the scale model were obsolete when tried on the hollow tubing this afternoon. The solid plastic took the light much more uniformly and was much easier to control than the hollow tubes, which acted like an array of convex lenses on the outside and concave lenses on the inside. Every flicker of light could be picked up by the back of the tube while the front would reject the same light source. Bates had tried every angle possible. No one had ever seen anything like Balanchine's "crystal ice palace."

Martins has been on stage and gazing up at a square trim of tubing. His new ballet, *Capriccio Italien*, a premiere tonight, will have no diagonals or arches in the setting. "There is not much I can do at this point," Bates tells the young choreographer as they stand unmoving against the working crew. Martins knows that the rest of the program has to be lit and looks anxious. Bates persuades him to hang on a few minutes more so he can set some "essentials." Robbins and Kirstein are already near Bates' desk, sitting in line with Ter-Arutunian. Balanchine joins their group. Bates and Martins return.

Bates is now in a better position to satisfy the artistic wishes of those around him and blend them with the technical capabilities of the set.

"The light should look like it is coming from above the center," Kirstein suggests. All the overhanging lights are brought up, partially achieving the desired effect. Experimenting, Bates calls for the pinks to be taken out of the ceiling lights.

"No! We need pinks for people!" Balanchine says.

"What happened to the side lights?" Martins questions. Bates starts to say that Balanchine and Kirstein wanted only center lights, but holds off. He is trying as many possibilities as time allows. Nothing is being set for Martins' ballet per se; unfortunately, the setting of the stage in general is the priority now. The rehearsal is two hours behind schedule and the scenery and lights a day. By the end of his ballet, Martins has managed to make it understood that he wants a subtle change in lighting—pastoral in one section, bright in another.

As *Mozartiana* is to start, the lights are more developed, with Bates and the crew understanding their problems just a bit better.

Balanchine climbs onto the stage and shows the women, large and small, how to wear tighter buns with their jeweled hairpieces. He puts his hand on the side of Fedorova's head where he wants their buns to be moved from their usual positions in the back. "Otherwise, you're like a car. You can't tell if it's going forward or backward." Farrell's costume has arrived only minutes ago.

Balanchine suggests Bates kill all the front lights. The floor is much darker but the tubes look spectacular. "This is the way it should be," bursts out Kirstein. "Dazzle, dazzle, dazzle." Balanchine, back in his seat, agrees.

"We have lit only the scenery now," says the stage manager. Balanchine gives the cue to start.

"It's your ballet," Bates warns; "we won't see any dancers." In response, Kirstein suggests more overheads from the bridge. The cherrypicker is wheeled in and a few more units and amber gels that color the lights are added.

Upstairs tomorrow's ballets are in rehearsal: the theater is running at full speed.

The beautiful song of the *Preghiera* section begins. Balanchine is back onstage snapping his fingers and directing the children; Robbins suggests to Bates some lighting for Balanchine's ballet while the choreographer pushes the children upstage. To save her toes, Farrell is not dancing full out. The choreographer returns to his seat and calls out directions to his dancers, but he cannot be heard. Seeing this, Robbins repeats Balanchine's directions over the mike, and asks the children not to go too far to the sides, and leave the lit part of the stage. Farrell asks if the lights will remain as is. No one answers.

177

Balanchine is back onstage desperately trying to express himself through the chaos. Dunleavy calms him and he returns to the audience, giving one last direction for the dancers to finish further upstage.

By the end of the *gigue* Balanchine is back onstage again, warning the *menuet* dancers to enter on the last six, seven, eight of d'Amboise's solo. With Dunleavy calling out corrections from the side, Balanchine shows the right positions for their heads and arms. A dozen photographers, lined up against the orchestra railing, click like excited sparrows. In silhouetted gestures, the young women repeat and Balanchine returns to his chair. Halfway through their dance, he asks Robbins to continue to watch the lighting. He does not need to return to the audience to maintain his perspective of what is seen onstage. "I have to tell them how to dance."

On the stage, Balanchine wends through the *menuet*, almost oblivious of time and consequence, as he decides exactly whether the dancers should *plié* on count one or two before a *sauté*. As he waits, Bates searches for the right combinations of light sources to produce attractive effects. Ever watchful, Robbins suggests, "I think you have to do that all over the place, because one place just takes your eye to it." The preliminary cue is fixed accordingly, and the stage becomes instantly luminous.

Andersen's costume has color. With everyone else in black and white, his Prussian blue velvet vest—over billowing white sleeves and ruffled shirt—and light blue tights almost look out of place. It complements Farrell's, however, which is less severe than the solid black costumes of the corps. As they turn to take their places upstage, the vermilion of the back of his vest is like a splash of warm light. When they dance their variations through, it doesn't seem to be so bold—instead, it is like a chuckle in a witty conversation or a delightful surprise.

Suddenly, during the *pas de deux*, a tinkling sounds from

way above the stage. The overhanging tubes are knocking into one another and begin to sway. Fearing they may fall, the dancers stop, ready to run. Bates calls in alarm up to the flyman.

The giant air conditioners have been turned on to cool the theater for the performance, now only two hours away. Bates instructs the crew to find the industrial fans used for the blizzard in *Nutcracker* and face them in the opposite direction of the air conditioners. By the time the fans are found, placed up in the catwalks and turned on, the air conditioners have automatically shut off but are left where they might fight future air currents. The dress rehearsal of *Mozartiana* progresses to an end.

Ter-Arutunian joins Balanchine onstage afterward. The choreographer points to a little bow on Farrell's bodice that he wants raised. The dancers are through. A cocktail party for the patrons is already under way on the grand promenade out in the lobby. Bates has not had time to decorate with old sets as he has for galas in the past.

The set definitely won't be hung completely. The lights are still a mystery to control. Robbins' ballet, *Pas de Deux*, has not been lit or set, although it begins a minute after the end of *Mozartiana*.

"Let's go with what you've already got," he tells Bates. "I only have two people. So I don't have to spread the lights all over the place. Go back to Peter's set. . . . How long will it take to change?"

"Only a moment."

The arches of tubes for *Mozartiana* are carefully raised and the square-topped trim of *Capriccio Italien* is brought in.

"I want the wings all the way off."

"Yes, sir," says Bates, getting his second wind. He will need it for the long night ahead.

179

THE GALA
PERFORMANCE

⌐ই⌐

The stage crew works on the lights until curtain time. The last ballet, *Tempo di Polacca,* has not had a costume or lighting rehearsal. The usually highly detailed cues, which were written, copied and filed for every ballet in the repertoire, are scribbles on legal pads, distributed only to controllers of the auxiliary electrical "specials" panel. The follow spot and the flymen don't have any. The stage is only swept, not mopped.

The dancers are also cramped for time—they have to clean off the rehearsal sweat, apply makeup and warm up without draining too much energy. The children are kept from getting into their costumes too soon and possibly dirtying them on the numerous trunks, crates, and light units backstage. But they have food from their mothers before they finally get to apply their makeup, supervised by the company makeup artist. Most dancers don't eat before performance, and if they do it's light—snacks of yogurt or honey.

Backstage the corridors are filled with the cacophony from blasts of brass, flurries of strings, and squeaks of reeds, and two singers caterwauling. Farrell, in full makeup and dressed in her theater robe, is holding on to a portable barre in the huge area offstage right; she is invigorated by backstage. In contrast, Andersen is warming up in a quiet corner of the Main Hall.

The crew can barely stand. The flymen have packed one hundred tons of counterweights and hoisted one hundred tons of tubing and overhead lights; they can hardly lift their arms. Bates, usually dressed impeccably by this time, has on yesterday's clothes. Incongruous, Kirstein, stooped and grand in his black suit, walks through the chaos—his aura creating tranquility. Sincerity and dedication to art have formed a brotherhood between him and Balanchine strong enough to withstand the whims of fifty years.

Balanchine stands close to the curtain talking to Irving. They watch the orchestra set up, until Bates calls "places." Soon the houselights dim, and the footlights come up. One can feel the audience inhale. But the curtain only parts in the middle. Irving inches out, holding one edge of the heavy golden cloth. He finally lets go of the curtain, puts on his reading glasses, produces paper from the pocket of his waistcoat. His speech is full of humor and musical insight. A rush of applause and the curtain rises. The orchestra is seated in a grand crescent. Years ago Balanchine was the first choreographer in America to demand quality musicians in an orchestra for anything other than opera, and now his splendid ballet orchestra was on stage.

The crinkled Mylar looks just like what it is, a wrinkled set. Unfortunately, the lights, focused for the transparent tubing, now fall on the solid unreflecting wrinkles. The soprano, Karen Hunt, strides to center, her silver gown clashing with the mercury colored set. She has not had a dress rehearsal.

Irving raises his baton and the orchestra begins. Hunt's voice sounds as full as it did in the afternoon, but is more expressive. The tenor's aria was impressive. Next a fragment that Tchaikovsky saved from his ill-fated opera *Undine* is performed in Russian. Balanchine had come across the lost words to this love duet in his regular studies of music. The famous scrap is the recurring theme in the second act of *Swan Lake*. Balanchine wanted to surprise, and he gets his reaction —a gasp of recognition passes through the audience. Lauded with applause, the two singers take their final bow. Now the orchestra fills the theater with glorious sound. Tchaikovsky's *Romeo and Juliet* Fantasy Overture is welcomed. The crowd sends back a tumultuous tribute. Backstage, Kirstein and Boelzner heartily congratulate Irving, the three of them un-characteristically effusive. Everyone receives the dancer's good luck gesture of two kissed fingers on the neck and, "Merde."

Ter-Arutunian is sewing the bows on d'Amboise's heeled shoes because they had been put on at the wrong angle. Bates and Tyler double-check their cues. Silvey is warning the dancers not to go onstage while the sets are being changed— the very first time they have not been allowed onstage while the crew is setting up. So much is unknown about the set that all precautions for injury are being taken. Just a few minutes before, one of the tubes forming the rear wall came unhooked and fell just a few inches from the stage. Any one of the thousands higher up could go too.

Balanchine is ushered offstage. He appears unperturbed, but he cares more than anyone else. Richardson bends over to encourage his troupe, who suddenly are attacked by nerves. The quartet of older women are already aware of the power of this momentous occasion.

Bates taps the conductor on the shoulder. "Robert, please," he says, and the conductor returns to the pit.

"Places, please," Silvey calls out.

Balanchine stands downstage right.

The chandelier slowly loses its glitter and the audience flutters to silence as Irving steps onto the podium. He bows to the warmth that greets him and asks the orchestra to rise. Having checked the monitor of the focused camera under the lip of the stage, Bates gives his cue for the curtain. It rises.

The perimeter of the stage is shrouded in blue and the center glows in amber. The plastic tubes have now been transformed into giant organ pipes in a heavenly cathedral. Farrell and the four girls stand immobile. Hushed clapping drifts over them. And then Irving begins.

The music seems to come from far away. Although Farrell is completely still, she appears to grow mysteriously. Her spirituality is offset by the four children. Their smallness lends a surreal effect—as if they are young women and Farrell a supernatural being. Glimmering as she moves forward, the ballerina slightly opens her arms in the sign of the cross, beseeching. She glides under the altar of crystal. Like flying birds the children slip past her as if she were an angel. Farrell then kneels and bares her throat in prayer. She rises to the swell of His response and swoons. Dressed in mourning black she floats through a mist, communing with the music. Finally she is still again, her arms extended heavenward, as the last three bowings of strings linger. All breath is gone.

Irving clears his eyes as the applause, almost sacrilegious, pours forth. D'Amboise runs to center stage and strikes his first pose. His infectious smile draws everyone back to the theater. In his costume of sheer black tights, satin knickers, a ruffled white shirt and a rib-length black jacket, he is perfectly elegant. No one could seem delicate immediately after Farrell's dance—d'Amboise does the only sensible thing and emphasizes the contrast. He meets the challenge. His exuberance, the clarity of his complicated footwork and timely bounds, halt with a spontaneous burst of applause and the arrival of the *menuet* dancers.

The four women extend their shapely limbs to the limit, and curve their arms over their sweetly tilted heads. They are poised, as Balanchine always told them to be, as if they were going to be kissed. Their faces show their pleasure. As they dance circles, squares and form tableaus, they seem many more than four. In this formal *menuet* Balanchine blends the lushest of movements with the most mannered. It finishes in a regal *révérence*.

The audience knows it is witnessing a very special ballet.

Irving now sets the pulse to the heart of the ballet. Nobly, Andersen leads Farrell, no longer an angel but a queen, down center.

They dance the variations as never before, but as Balanchine knew they could. The essence of each is revealed. The ballerina is so at ease, so fluid, so in command of her technique, yet yields to everyone's fantasy. Balanchine's complex understanding of Tchaikovsky's work is enhanced.

Andersen dances the performance of his life. In just ten minutes the role becomes his signature. He has summoned his strength to gain finesse. Covering the stage with leaps and intricate brilliance, his spirit sparkles like a star. The audience holds its breath. His *pirouettes* are impeccable; and even though Irving takes his last variation at a demandingly slow tempo, the dancer surpasses the highest expectations.

Anticipation fills the theater as the inevitable *pas de deux* will have Andersen and Farrell perform together for the first time.

But suddenly something seems wrong with Farrell. She looks concerned; and every so often a step is flawed. Beneath her regal air, it seems her confidence is gone. By the end of their dance, though, her doubts seem to have vanished as mysteriously as they came.

D'Amboise's pose with the four young girls has zest. With swelling pride, the young girls match the exuberance of d'Amboise and the music. The young women return and shower the space with their loveliness before Andersen and Farrell rejoin them. Again her pose seems unsure, but she twirls about the stage with the clarinet and opens fully into the final celebration.

The four little girls grasp Farrell's and Andersen's hands,

ready to dance with professional style. No longer children, they prance step for step alongside the ballerina who has possessed the greatest understanding of Balanchine's genius.

The dream of Lincoln Kirstein and George Balanchine that was first discussed in London in 1933 has just been fulfilled. It was the dream of developing a ballet company and a school of equal quality, which would create an institution of dance as glorious as any of the past. Dara Adler, Lisa Cantor, Amy Fixler and Tamara Molina may never develop into great ballerinas, but tonight they have made history. For the first time in a ballet of the New York City Ballet, young students are not in children's roles but are integral to a ballet's design.

The final tableau is dazzlingly full of feelings and ideas, dreams and fancies: a Balanchine world.

The audience applauds for a long time, causing the usual vibrations in the feet of the dancers standing onstage. Andersen and Farrell hug each other behind the curtain when it lowers for the last time. Outside, a circle of press and photographers surround the three choreographers represented tonight. Lincoln Kirstein is within his own circle of balanced peace. A smile wets his face as his eyes rest on Balanchine.

After the following performances, in which Andersen and Darci Kistler sweep through Robbins' *Pas de Deux*, the advanced students from the school dance admirably in Martins' *Capriccio Italien*. Farrell valiantly returns with Martins in a grande finale; later it is learned that Farrell had dislocated a bone in her foot.

Most of the company celebrate at the gala party, but there is still much to do. The *Pathétique* has not yet been touched; other ballets still need tinkering. Tomorrow, *Mozartiana* will have to be replaced by the shorter *Capriccio Italien* and *Pas de Deux*. Many programs will have to be changed because of Farrell's injury. And every ballet within the next two weeks has to be set with new lighting and scenic design, before it is all put aside for the repertory season. Change and development are what has kept Balanchine and his troupe vital.

Much later on the night of June 4, the auditorium is dark. The stage is bare. One work light shines on the center. Only shadows remain. Balanchine has left the theater for home.

Afterword

────────────────── ₹❧ ──────────────────

A few days after the performance of *Mozartiana*, Maiorano approached Balanchine backstage and asked if he had any feelings about his newest work.

"Bobby you should know better," he said quietly, "I have no feelings. I am like a prop—necessary. I am like that trunk over there," he pointed, "It doesn't feel. It is a part. It is in place. Everyday, I am here in theater, in my place."

Injuries plagued Farrell and Andersen throughout the summer and due to the cancelled performances, an aura of mystery and curiosity surrounded the rare ballet. Yet since then, *Mozartiana* has drawn many devotees and has gained an honored place in the repertoire alongside such epochal ballets as *Apollo, Serenade, Four Temperaments, Symphony in C, Orpheus* and *Agon. Mozartiana* is already a symbolic requiem. For it has proven to be Balanchine's last completed work, which was not officially or unofficially shared by another choreographer, nor has it became *un piece d'occasion* such as the moving *Adagio Lamentosa* of the "Pathétique" Symphony at the end of the Tchaikovsky Festival, or the *Elegy* rede-

187

veloped for Farrell in the Stravinsky Centennial Celebration the following spring.

In the fall of 1982 Balanchine was stricken with what doctors eventually discovered was one of the world's most unusual diseases—Creutzfeldt-Jakob, a slow virus with an extremely long incubation period. He died April 30, 1983 of pneumonia. On that day Lincoln Kirstein, in a cracked voice, told a crying handful of dancers before class that Balanchine died this Day of Lazarus, the day Christ raised Lazarus from the grave, ". . . and our continued dancing would lift Balanchine." Before the curtain rose, he managed to say to the audience, "Balanchine is with Mozart, Tchaikovsky and Stravinsky. . . ."